Praise for "But What If I Live? The American Retirement Crisis"

"Dr. Salsbury's book offers common sense solutions for those who want to avoid America's retirement crisis. It is destined to become the bible for anyone intereste[...] [...]nt."

Professor John P. Huggard, J.D., CFP®, CLU, ChFC
Department of Business Management
North Carolina State University

"This book is such a wonderful compendium of historical and [...] information that it should be read and kept on every book shelf."

Donald Ray Haas, CLU, ChFC, CFP®, RFC, MSFS
Author of "Financial Planning for the Baby Boomer Client" & "Money Forever"

"An exceptional resource that details the threats facing both boomers and retirees, and provides a needed wake-up call for consumers to act today to safeguard their future years. I believe this easy-to-read book will be popular with both clients and financial advisers."

Jack Marrion
Financial Author, Publisher and President of Advantage Compendium, Ltd.

"It is hard for young people who want it all now to listen to the voice of their future old self. Gregory Salsbury reminds us that most people need all the help they can get from employers, financial advisers and the government to quiet the voice of the young and bolster the voice of the old."

Professor Meir Statman
Department of Finance
Santa Clara University

"Greg Salsbury delivers harsh facts and simple solutions in a book that should propel readers to stop spending and start saving for retirement."

Ed Slott, CPA
Retirement Planning Expert and Author of "Parlay Your IRA Into a Family Fortune"

But What If I Live?

The American Retirement Crisis®

A Retirement Guide for Baby Boomers

P.O. Box 14367
Cincinnati, OH 45250-0367
www.NationalUnderwriterStore.com
800-543-0874 – 859-692-2100

The A Unit of Highline Media
National Underwriter Company
The Leader in Insurance and Financial Services Information

Gregory Salsbury, Ph.D.

ISBN 0-87218-697-0

1st Edition
4th Printing

Printed in U. S. A.

Dedication

To 'The Bear,' who managed to raise a family of six, retire early and pack more fun into 77 years than most people could in a century.

To my lovely wife Marian, who, with grace and competence, has managed a young and growing household through multiple relocations, outrageous travel schedules and demanding projects such as this one.

Acknowledgements

I would like to extend my thanks and appreciation to the following people who contributed to the creation of this book:

C. Philip Wright
Don Glover
Scott Donnell
Doug Mantelli
Peter Radloff, JD
James Marshall
Nick Walsh

Table of Contents

Prologue

Before his passing a couple of months ago, I told my father, who was 78, that I was writing a book about the American retirement crisis. He nodded enthusiastically, as it was a topic he and I had discussed frequently over the last decade. Most often, our conversations on the subject tended to revolve around the question of how difficult it would be for subsequent generations to enjoy an equal or greater quality of retirement life as compared to his generation. America is a country that has prided itself on continual improvement and, indeed, in so many ways — from technology to social progress — we are light years ahead of where we were a half-century or more ago. But as my father and I analyzed the dozens of variables that go into calculating post-employment life here in the U.S., we were increasingly led to the conclusion that the answer would not be nearly so clear. In fact, it seemed clear to us that for many Americans, steps backward in this department were almost inescapable.

Up until the last five years or so, my dad's retirement seemed to unfold nicely, and he certainly wouldn't have considered his own situation to be problematic, much less in crisis. You see, my father worked for an engineering and aircraft company for more than 30 years and retired at the age of 58. For the first 10 years or so, his retirement went pretty smoothly — until his company pension plan decided that they hadn't promised lifetime healthcare benefits after all. Following that event, retirement for my father and mother became a lot tighter financially, as they began the ongoing process of assessing, selecting, and sometimes changing health coverage plans. But despite this notable exception, he enjoyed 20 wonderful years in retirement.

My dad and I estimated that he had probably collected a fair amount more in Social Security benefits than he contributed throughout his working life — similar to many other Americans in his generation. In fact, wage earners from my father's generation may have collected anywhere from seven to twenty times more than they contributed to Social Security, depending on income. Future generations of retirees may not be so lucky. My dad's generation lived through their share of crises: The Great Depression, several wars and potential nuclear disasters, the social upheaval of the '60s, the oil embargo and double digit inflation rates just to name a few.

But retirement wasn't typically one of them.

I am aware that within this book, I am primarily addressing a middle or upper-middle class reader. With regard to its retirement situation, our country is currently bifurcated between the mass and middle markets, and the wholly unprepared. The latter group faces a dismal situation indeed. But this book is not directed at this group — although it is certainly a deserving focus as well. Some 40 percent of America has saved nothing at all for retirement.[1] The retirement future for this group will be largely determined by their ability to keep working, and by governmental assistance. Most of the remaining 60 percent have saved some, but not enough. It is this latter group upon which the book focuses. These are the folks who still have the power to influence the type of retirement they will enjoy — or not.

Many people of my father's generation were quite a bit worse off financially than he was, and many worked until they died. But people in these same economic classes today will discover a far more challenging retirement situation — some of it psychological, and pertaining to their own expectations, and some of it quite physical, and simply fiscal.

Recently, National Public Radio aired a story about Social Security and retirement in America. They interviewed a 94-year-old woman named Helen who pointed out that, in her day, most people worked until they died. And if they couldn't work any longer, they moved in with relatives. She recounted how this was the case for her own grandfather who had run a neighborhood grocery store up until his death in his 60s. At this point, her grandmother came to live with them in their tiny apartment in the Bronx.

That was the norm then. Prior to World War II, it was customary for elderly Americans to live with their children given the absence of a formal retirement structure. A lengthy, leisurely and well-funded retirement was an experience reserved exclusively for the most affluent.

What we call "retirement" is an invention, like the light bulb or the automobile. In its current form, the American concept of retirement has only been around since 1935 with the New Deal and the founding of Social Security. This legislation helped give millions of Americans both leisure time and money as no other generation of Americans had experienced. To be clear, they weren't wealthy, and life expectancies were still well below today's, but still, it was a luxury previously unknown on that scale.

As with any invention, retirement has undergone changes in concept, design, benefits and even availability. I think we're all aware of the evolution and sophistication of retirement plans, the constant threats to raise the retirement age and, of course, the changing images of what retirement life should look like. The modern concept of retirement began with small pensions paid to government officials, military veterans, widows and orphans, and has developed into a pervasive industrial model. Retirement is supposed to mean that you can stop working at a given age, typically 65, and be supported by "something" — the return on your investments, savings, pensions and payments from government-sponsored programs such as Social Security.

In conversations with a lot of my boomer colleagues, I have found that they embrace a sort of romantic illogic on this issue. And if pressed on the topic, many will admit that they can't identify what their "something" will be. They seem to subconsciously expect to retire in good health, and go on living the same lifestyle or even better for another 20 years — supported in some way by a sort of defined benefit program (often because so many previous retirees in their families enjoyed these). Never mind that their current employer doesn't have one of those, and that American employees covered by such a thing have become about as rare as someone who still balances a checkbook. Never mind all that. They go on living as if some philanthropist is going to hand them a check each month after they turn 65.

My father managed at least 20 mostly enjoyable years of retirement. But my profound worry is that ours will be the first generation in mass that will be worse off in retirement than the generation before. Or said another way, the Boomers may have to work dramatically harder to achieve roughly the same standard of living in retirement as the previous generation.

I think it's fair to say that I'm financially and materially better off than my father was at my age (even in inflation-adjusted dollars), and probably any generation in my family before him — just as he would have both hoped and expected. But I also spend much more than my parents ever did. For instance, I drive an expensive SUV, will pay to have it washed and detailed, pay someone to spend 15 minutes cutting my lawn and picking up twigs, have a dry cleaner who both picks up and delivers to my front door, stay at fairly nice hotels, and yes, on occasion, I have been known to pay too much for a gourmet cup of coffee.

My parents, on the other hand, held on to the same car for years, and wouldn't have dreamt of paying to have it washed regularly, let alone detailed. And don't even mention laying down seven dollars for brown liquid and a low-fat apricot muffin. They kept every National Geographic ever mailed to them, old television cabinets from which the tube had long been gone and snow tires from a 1968 Chrysler.

Both of my parents lived through the Great Depression. My mother, in particular, had it tough. She survived war-torn Germany, where she endured long periods with nothing to eat but bacon grease spread on toast. My father talked about saving string from the evening paper, re-using the wax paper packaging from loaves of bread for baking and how he had carried a lunch pail into adulthood. Me? I get upset when we run out of Brie.

My father worked the bulk of his career without the need to put in 70-hour weeks — he was nearly always home in time for 6 p.m. dinner. He didn't have a Blackberry affixed to his belt — a work-related call in the evening or on weekends was an oddity, or heavy business travel — his nights away from home in a given year were typically fewer than a dozen, and these trips were often considered perks, especially when they involved air travel. My mother worked part-time on and off, but her chief motivation for doing so was not financial. Yet gone are the days, for the most part, when a single wage-earner (Dad) could support a family of four or five, come home for dinner — on time — every night and help the children with their homework before getting plenty of sleep for the next day's work.

Today, in many families, both parents work outside the home. There are more dual-income families in America than ever before. What was once considered a "traditional household," comprised of a working father and a mother who stayed at home and cared for the children, is now almost non-existent. In fact, only 7 percent of households currently fall into that category,[2] and this fact has led to a decline in leisure time even for the more affluent. Parents spend time ferrying their kids to music lessons and soccer games, when they are not working 60 hours a week at their hectic corporate jobs or businesses. Just ask yourself how often are you home to have dinner with your family and you may start to wonder if your life is truly better than the lives of your parents. You probably have to work a lot harder for the security that generations before you had, and yet you'll still be lucky if you have the retirement your parents had.

In June of 2006, USA Today ran two related stories. The first was the lead cover page story entitled "*In Debt Before You Start*" about the soaring number of college graduates owing more than $100K by the time they get out of school, and looking at loan payments with durations typical of a home mortgage. The other was a little article on the third page of the Money section proclaiming, "*Lunch Break Becomes Briefer As 'hour' Shrinks*." It pointed out that the average lunch break in America has shrunk by a full 14 percent just since 1996 to a mere 31 minutes, and most Americans now eat lunch at their desks as they work. What's the connection between higher education costs and shorter lunch breaks? It seems harder to get and stay ahead today. It costs more. More money and more sweat equity. Accordingly, the lengthy, leisurely and luxurious retirement envisioned by many Americans will become increasingly elusive.

Every successive generation of Americans over the last century has been more prosperous and has enjoyed a better quality of life and a better retirement. Every generation has seen an improvement — until now. But at the same time, retirement didn't used to be a problem — until now. To paraphrase a line from Oldsmobile, "This is not your parents' retirement." The trouble is many boomers don't seem to know that retirement, if we have one, may be inferior to their parents', yet no one seems worried. And no one is taking action. Ready or not, the first wave of Baby Boomers has arrived, as 2.8 million Americans, including President Bush, turn 60 this year (2006).

Throughout this book, we're going to explore the seven key challenges that stand between you and a successful retirement. Understanding these challenges and taking action to overcome their impact on retirement could help you avoid a financially insecure retirement and a substandard lifestyle. Let's take a quick look at what could tarnish your "Golden Years," and what you might do about it.

1. Aging of America

According to Cerulli Associates, in the next 20 years, 43 million households, nearly half of all American households, will move into retirement, pushing the number of 65+ year olds to more than 69 million people. Since 1900, the average life expectancy of Americans has nearly doubled. The Society of Actuaries just increased the top age of its mortality chart from 100 years to 120 years.[3] And for a 65-year-old couple, the odds that one spouse will live until age 90 are over 50 percent.

2. Disappearing Pensions

About 44 million Americans are covered by pension plans, yet the number of these plans is plummeting.[4] In fact, each year, more than 1,000 employers voluntarily shut down their pension plans, leaving a shrinking pool of employers paying into the federal retirement insurance program. Consequently, the number of employer-sponsored pension plans has declined precipitously, from 114,000 in 1985 to 28,769 in 2005.[5]

In spring 2005, a U.S. bankruptcy judge approved a proposal from the United Airlines parent, UAL Corp., to transfer four underfunded employee pension plans to the federal government, paving the way for the largest pension default thus far in U.S. history.

3. Social Insecurity

The federal government currently owes Social Security over $1.5 trillion; without a tax increase or a reduction in benefits, Social Security marches toward bankruptcy. Yet according to the Social Security Administration, nearly two-thirds of retirees rely on Social Security for 50 percent of their income, and 33 percent use it for 90 percent of their income. Without Social Security, half of retirees would live in poverty.

4. The Tax Axe

What is your family's largest monthly expense? Typical answers include: Housing, food, healthcare, transportation, etc. Nope. Did you know that taxes are the single greatest monthly expense for most American families, accounting for 30 percent of their income — almost twice as much as the next expense category? That amount surprises most people. But aren't the taxes always going up on the rich? Well, yes, pretty much true. So, won't the rich bail you out? Well, here's another shock: "They" is you. You may not consider yourself rich, but if your household earned $57,343 in 2003, that puts you squarely in the top 25 percent of all taxpayers in America.[6]

5. The Invisible Enemy — Inflation

You may have forgotten about inflation, but inflation has not forgotten about you. Inflation is truly the invisible enemy of your income. It eats away at your purchasing power and can decrease the value of your assets. For example, if you need $50,000 a year in today's dollars, you will need $65,239 in 10 years, and $101,640 in 25 years. And these amounts would just maintain your standard of living, not increase it.

6. The Healthcare Nightmare

While the White House and the media continue to focus on Social Security, the real "gorilla in the closet" is healthcare, a problem with no proposed solution. In fact, in 2005, elder care replaced child care as the number one dependent care in U.S. households.[7] And finally, the Employee Benefits Research Institute (EBRI) estimates that, even with Medicare, the average American will need almost $300,000 in inflation adjusted dollars just to pay Medicare premiums in retirement.

And let's be honest with ourselves now …

7. Red, White and Broke

In going through my father's paperwork after his death, we were perplexed by thousands of dollars in cash found in one of his desk drawers, along with a journal indicating monthly additions to his stash. Turns out that he was saving for a new car, and intended to pay for it the way he had always paid for such things — in cash, cash that had been saved in advance. The monthly sums, as it turns out, were precisely the amount he calculated would equal a standard loan payment on the vehicle. If only more of America had such saving discipline.

In 2005, America's savings rate hit its lowest point since the Great Depression.[8] Personal bankruptcies hit an all time high.[9] Social Security was the major source of income (providing at least 50 percent of total income) for 65 percent of aged beneficiaries, and it was the only source of income for 21 percent[10] — and remember that's an IOU, not a savings account. Given these challenges, and the lack of preparation by investors, it is quite possible that many boomers, perhaps you, will enter retirement with the very real prospect of running out of money. I am glad your busy schedule allows you the time to read this book. I hope that, male or female, you arrived home at six o'clock this evening, hung up your coat and called out, "Honey, I'm home!" And I hope you're now ready to confront the major retirement crisis in your life.

Good. Let's talk about it.

[1] Employee Benefit Research Institute.

[2] AmeriStat, data from the 2002 Current Population Survey (March Supplement).

[3] "The Looming Retirement Income Crisis," On Wall Street (June 2004).

[4] Greg Crawford and Vineeta Anand, "The Looming Retirement Disaster," *Pensions and Investments*, April 18, 2005.

[5] Pension Insurance Data Book, 2005.

[6] "Summary of Federal Individual Income Tax Data," Tax Foundation, *www.taxfoundation.org*, October 11, 2005.

[7] Don Kuhn, "Part II: Shopping for Long Term Care Insurance" (April 2003).

[8] "Gold: There's No Free Lunch." John Ing. March 30, 2006.

[9] "Personal Bankruptcies Soar To All-Time High," *CNN Money.com*, March 24, 2006.

[10] Fast Facts & Figures About Social Security, 2005.

Introduction ◄
The Retirement Landscape

An Historical Perspective

According to the Online Etymology Dictionary, the word "retire" was first used in connection with the sense of "leave an occupation" in 1648.[1] This use implied retirement, but the simple fact is that retirement — i.e., leaving a job and stopping work — is a relatively new concept. If you examine the ancient cultures of Mesopotamia, Babylonia, Egypt and Rome, you will find that older adults just didn't retire. The older generations were highly respected and were often given jobs more suitable to their physical abilities and accumulated wisdom, but they did not stop working. While there is some evidence that governments did provide some support for older soldiers and workers for the state, especially in Egypt, people simply did not retire the way we do today.[2]

It's not exactly clear when the concept of retirement actually began, but we know that in the 1880s German Chancellor Otto von Bismarck set the retirement age in Germany at 65. Since life expectancy at the time was only 45 years, this may seem somewhat laughable, but it does demonstrate the concept of retirement for an older population.

In the U.S., the word "retirement" first appeared in the 1828 edition of Webster's American Dictionary. In the original definition, there was no mention of leaving a job due to old age. Retirement simply meant a "state of being withdrawn." And though individual pieces, such as pension plans, of what would later be a part of retirement plans, began to emerge in the late 19th century, the word "retiree" did not appear in recorded usage until 1945. So when Americans first stopped working and began to draw an income from company pensions, Social Security, and whatever they might have invested into private accounts, they were doing something that had little precedence in world history.

Retirement in the U.S.

At the nation's founding, most Americans lived in rural areas. They supported themselves on farms, remaining self-sufficient and requiring little in the way of income or support from anyone except family members. There was no need for a social system to support people in their old age, because families on their farms

For old folks with no family, it was quite common for them to be sent to the county poorhouse.

were already taking responsibility; this agricultural model is still in place in many parts of the world. Also, in those days, city dwellers would provide grandpa and grandma with a room in the family house or apartment. And for old folks with no family, it was quite common for them to be sent to the county poorhouse, where they were thrown in with other charity cases like orphans, unwed mothers and the mentally ill.

One of the earliest examples of retirement in America came in the form of government-mandated pension payments. These funds were given to veterans or their widows after armed conflicts, including the Revolutionary War and the Civil War. By the end of the 19th century, many innovative companies had developed formal pension plans. Some even had mandatory retirement. Into the early 20th century, most state governments had passed retirement provisions for teachers. Some states provided limited pensions for poor, elderly residents.

But as the new century advanced, farmers' children were drawn to the cities to find work in the factories of the expanding industrial society. The concept of retirement grew in popularity, because of the nature of factory labor. Sheer physical strength was required to do the hard work. As workers grew older, their diminished physical skills left them unable to do their jobs; workers began to demand greater retirement benefits.

In 1935 Social Security came into being as part of the New Deal. The program was eventually enhanced with survivor benefits, cost-of-living increases and Medicare benefits. Social Security's initial purpose was to solve the problem of unemployment, as well as help keep the elderly spending and contributing to the economy. In fact, prior to the creation of *Older Americans were now "senior citizens." A retirement culture grew and thrived.* Social Security there was a movement to reduce the eight-hour workday to a six-hour workday in order to make room for all the unemployed being created by the Great Depression. But this movement was pitted against another movement that eventually won out — keep the eight-hour day but force people to retire at 65.

After World War II, and continuing into the 1970s, private pensions increased in popularity, covering nearly 30 percent of the labor force. During the '60s a "retirement boom" took over the country's consciousness. Older Americans were now "senior citizens." A retirement culture grew and thrived with new housing communities, leisure activities, retirement homes and marketing programs for the newly minted seniors.[3]

But in the 1970s and '80s, America began to lag behind other countries in retirement planning, benefits and even solvency. Social Security was built on an unsustainable platform that was starting to rust at the edges. Foreign competition was driving America out of its world-leading market position. The dual evils of recession and inflation combined to lower real incomes. This fiscal pressure led to financial crises, such as pension defaults in several large cities, as well as corporate bankruptcies.

Even Social Security was changed by Congress, and not necessarily for the better: there was a delay in a cost-of-living adjustment; up to half of benefits became taxable; and, payroll taxes increased eventually to an amount 10 times the 1970 rate.

In the 1990s, partly because of the need for individuals to save for retirement, defined contribution pension plans like IRAs and 401(k)s became more popular as individual solutions to the perceived problems of relying too much on Social Security or even company pension plans.[4] But throughout much of American history, Social Security has been synonymous with retirement.

The Social Security Act of 1935

The most significant part of Franklin D. Roosevelt's New Deal was the 1935 Social Security Act — the motivation of which, however, has been misunderstood. Its purpose was not so much to provide a pension for the elderly, but rather to create an incentive for older workers to leave the workplace and make room for younger workers.

A Timeline History of Retirement in the United States

1781 – Government-provided pensions initiated for disabled veterans and widows in post-colonial era.

1916 – Thirty-three states had passed retirement provisions for teachers. Some states provided limited pensions to poor elderly residents. By the 1930s, 28 states had established similar pension programs.

1860 – Judges in some states forced into mandatory retirement.

1890 – Pension Act of 1890. Benefits for all Union Army veterans age 65 and over.

1935 – Social Security Act, part of New Deal.

1880s – Rise of corporations. Early corporate pension plans, such as the Pennsylvania Railroad's, were funded entirely by the employer, and were awarded after 30 years' service with mandatory retirement at age 70.

1940-1960 – The number of people covered by private pensions increased from 3.7 million to 23 million, or to nearly 30 percent of the labor force.

1828 – The word retirement first appears in Webster's American Dictionary.

1902 – At its peak, nearly 1 million pensioners in the Union Army vets program consumed about 30 percent of the federal budget.

1875 – American Express Company developed first formal pension.

1926 – Revenue Act excluded from current taxation all income earned in pension trusts. Gave incentive for firms to provide pensions. By 1930, a majority of large firms had adopted pension plans, covering 20 percent of all industrial workers.

1880 – Southern states began pensions for disabled Confederate veterans and for war widows.

1939 – Social Security survivor benefits provided to retiree's spouse and children.

Social Security was really a "jobs act" geared toward providing relief for the persistently high unemployment rate during the depths of the Great Depression. The choices were to shorten the workday so that more people could be employed or create a forced retirement at age 65. Retirement won out, so, in essence, the retirement wave was actually an unintended consequence of the Social Security Act.

With the advent of Social Security, the elderly, for the first time, had full knowledge of where their next dollar was coming from. Suddenly, there were millions of Americans who had both leisure time and money — as no other generation of Americans had experienced. They weren't really wealthy, but still, it was a leisure class that had never before existed.

The dream was being realized — Americans had money, health and a safety net. And the concept of retirement, as we know it today, began to take shape.

2042 – Social Security Fund projected to be exhausted.

1983 – Social Security changes included delay of a cost-of-living adjustment, taxation of up to half of benefits, and payroll tax increases.

2013 – Pension Benefit Guaranty Corporation (PBGC), the federal corporation that guarantees corporate pensions, will run out of funds.

1976 – Municipal pension defaults in several large cities.

2005 – United Airlines defaults on its pension plan. Some pensioners receive about 25 cents on the dollar.

1965 – Medicare added to Social Security Act.

1950-1975 – The retirement boom. Nursing homes, retirement communities, "senior citizen" culture thrived.

1977 – Formula for determining Social Security benefits adjusted downward.

2011 – First Baby Boomer, of 75 million born between 1946-1964, reaches traditional retirement age 65.

1968 – Social Security benefits were increased 13 percent, another 15 percent in 1969, and 20 percent in 1972.

1990s – Rise of defined contribution pension plans – IRA, 401(k).

2018 – Social Security will begin paying out more than it takes in.

The New Retirement Landscape

But just as all the pieces were coming together for Americans to live longer and healthier lives, collect their employer pensions and enjoy a governmental safety net to boot — the same pieces started falling apart.

The first piece to disappear was America's saving habit. Americans abandoned their frugal saving and spending habits learned from leaner times, like the Depression. This abandonment gave rise to different views between Baby Boomers and their parents toward saving and spending (as shown by the illustrations of behaviors characteristic of Boomers' parents and by the behaviors of Baby Boomers). In addition, as America aged, Social Security became increasingly unstable and healthcare costs skyrocketed. An increasing number of employers quit offering pension plans, while remaining plans cut benefits dramatically, and many fell into default. All of a sudden, it was up to individuals to take financial responsibility for their own well-being in retirement. Unlike many other parts of the world, Americans were left to fend for themselves in this regard, which is the challenge we are still facing today.

We have slowly been evolving to this point over the last 20 years as the burden of saving for retirement has been steadily shifting back to the individual. America's

A Different View Towards Spending and Saving

- Shopped at the "Five & Dime"
- Dined out only on her birthday
- Hid cash in her home
- Hated to turn on the air conditioner
- Covered couches in plastic
- Sewed patches on blue jeans
- Wouldn't pay to have her car washed
- Reused tea bags

retirement landscape is split between well-prepared, affluent households and the wholly unprepared. The latter are facing a dismal financial situation. Last year, America had record debt,[5] the lowest savings rate since the Great Depression,[6] and an all-time high for personal bankruptcies.[7]

The result? A generation that is undersaved, overspent (overborrowed) and unprepared for a comfortable retirement. Americans are facing a real retirement crisis.

Undersaved

The first major challenge facing retirees is that they are undersaved. Today, savings rates are at their lowest levels since the Great Depression. For the first time since 1933, the savings rate fell into negative territory at -0.5 percent in 2005. Americans either dipped into savings or increased their borrowing.[8]

- Forty percent of workers have saved nothing for retirement.[9]
- Nearly 28 million U.S. households — 37 percent of the total — do not have a retirement savings account of any kind.[10]
- The typical American household has saved only $18,750 for retirement.[11]

- Shops at Nordstrom
- Dines out frequently
- Stops daily at Starbucks
- Travels first class
- Leases a new car every two years
- Details his car regularly
- Vacations at resorts
- Buys the latest and greatest electronics

U.S. Savings Rate	
Time Period	**Savings Rate % of GDP**
1960s	11.0%
1970s	8.7%
1980s	6.2%
1990s	4.5%
2000s	<2.0%

Source: Peter G. Peterson, *Running on Empty*, Picador (2004)

Overspent

Unfortunately, many Americans also live well above their means, creating one of the most debt-laden societies ever witnessed.

• U.S. consumer debt has doubled over the past 10 years, with the average debt at $18,700 per U. S. household (excluding mortgages); bankruptcy filings are estimated to have topped 1.8 million in 2005.[12]

In January of 2002, the Employee Benefit Research Institute released its Retirement Risk Survey, highlighting the complete lack of savings in this country. When the accumulated savings and investments for retirees and pre-retirees were compared, the results were similar:[13]

• Almost three in ten (28 percent) say they have saved less than $50,000.
• Barely one in ten reports having saved $50,000-$99,999 (12 percent of retirees and 17 percent of pre-retirees).
• Roughly two in ten claimed to have saved between $100,000 and $250,000 (20 percent of retirees and 24 percent of pre-retirees).
• Less than one in ten have saved more than $250,000 (9 percent of retirees and 9 percent of pre-retirees).

But the crisis involves much more than simply a change in spending and savings values.

In the past, Americans' worst nightmare about retirement was not reaching it. They nervously asked, "What if I die before I retire, before I can enjoy my golden years?" But with rising longevity accompanied by astounding leaps in expenses, a more troubling question looms: "But what if I live? What if I live another 20, 30 or even 50 years after I retire? What if my body holds out, but my portfolio doesn't?"

The crisis is real, and it's lurking just around the corner. It concerns every American — both investors and advisers alike. And with every day that passes, it threatens to become worse. So, let's examine the mess we're in, and what we can do to get out of it.

[1] Douglas Harper, *Online Etymology Dictionary* (November 2001).

[2] Marie Parsons, "Old Age in Ancient Egypt," *www.touregypt.net*, October 4, 2005.

[3] Nancy R. Gibbs, "Grays on the Go," Time, February 22, 1988.

[4] Ken Dychtwald, "Why We're Outgrowing Retirement," *Yahoo! Finance*, September 23, 2005.

[5] Rob Kellen, "Debt, Consumers Juggle Big Burden," *money.cnn.com*, October 10, 2005.

[6] Philip Thornton, "US Savings Rate Sinks to Lowest Since Great Depression," *www.commondreams.org*, January 31, 2006.

[7] "Personal Bankruptcies Soar To All-Time High," *money.cnn.com*, March 24, 2006.

[8] Martin Crutsinger, "Savings Rate at Lowest Level Since 1933," *Associated Press*, January 30, 2006.

[9] The National Retirement Planning Coalition, 2004.

[10] Dan Ackman, "Retirement Doomsday," *Forbes.com*, May 4, 2005.

[11] Kathie O' Donnell, "Fidelity unveils retirement index," *Market Watch*, June 7, 2005.

[12] Timothy Egan, "Debtors in Rush to Bankruptcy as Change Nears," *The New York Times Online*, August 21, 2005.

[13] EBRI, Retirement Risk Survey (January 2002).

By 2030, the demographics of 32 states will resemble those of Florida today.

Chapter One ◀
Aging America

The Methuselah Generation

One of my favorite audience participation games during my retirement planning seminars is the *Methuselah* exercise. You may even want to try it yourself while you're reading. The exercise goes like this:

Speaker addresses audience:

How many of you know who Methuselah was? According to the *Bible* in Genesis, Chapter 5, verses 21 through 27, Methuselah was the oldest man of whom we have any record. He died at the age of 969 years, in the year of the Flood.

Now let's all stand up for a moment. Those of you who believe that you will die before age 60, sit down.

Okay, those who believe you will die before age 70, sit down.

Now, those who believe you will die before age 80, sit down. And those who believe you will die before age 90 sit down.

Still standing? How about 100? And beyond? Most of the time there is a room full of folks still standing. A room full of Methuselahs.

My guess is that many of you imagine yourselves to be like Methuselah as well. You are prepared to live a very long life, and as we'll discuss in this chapter, the likelihood of living longer has never been greater.

But how many of you are *financially* prepared to live that long?

The point is clear. Most of us hope to live a long life. Many of us even expect to. Your expectations for a long life may be perfectly reasonable.
But it's going to cost you. And you'd better be ready.

During the last century, our life expectancy has almost doubled. People are living longer and retiring earlier, so retirees face the very real prospect of outliving their savings. The average person can expect to live 19 or more years in retirement.[1] And not only are people living longer, but the proportion of our older population in this country is growing dramatically. America's Baby Boomers make up the largest demographic group in the country's history. And as they near retirement, they will reach the point where they should find themselves with increased control over their retirement assets. The next generation of retirees should be the healthiest, longest-lived, best educated and most affluent in history. But they are also aging.

Marching to Immortality?

The average life expectancy of Americans jumped more than 60% in the past century, with women recently crossing the mark of age 80.

Life Expectancies	■ Male ■ Female	Years
1900		46.3
		48.3
1950		65.6
		71.1
1960		66.6
		73.1
1970		67.1
		74.7
1980		70.0
		77.4
1990		71.8
		78.8
2000		74.3
		79.7
2003		74.8
		80.1

The Aging of the Aged

You may have heard the statistic that every eight seconds another American Baby Boomer turns 50. But the more telling statistic is that every 12 seconds an American turns 65. By the time the last Boomer hits 65,[2] a full 20 percent of the U.S. population — the largest proportion in American history — will be of retirement age.[3] And did you know that, by the year 2030, the number of Americans aged 55 and older will have almost doubled over what it is today?[4] In the United States, elderly people are the fastest growing portion of the population. The 80-and-over age group is growing five times faster than the overall population.[5] By 2030, the demographics of 32 states may resemble those of Florida today.[6]

These statistics force us to ask: How will Americans deal with the dramatic increase in the number of retirees?

Get a Bigger Turkey

In the past, people worried about providing for their parents. We've all joked about having a big enough turkey for Thanksgiving. But now it's not such a joke. Today, many people may face the challenge of providing for more than one generation of dependents, perhaps both their parents *and* their grandparents.

What concerns do most people have about aging?

They worry about getting sick.
They worry about outliving their money.
They worry about the uncertainty of their retirement future.

And worry they should; already in 2005, elder care replaced child care as the number-one dependent care in America.[7] And America's growing proportion of elderly is only part of a problem compounded by the fact that we are living longer than ever before. We have a polite word for this aging of the aged: longevity.

Longevity

For centuries, mankind has considered longevity as something rare, exotic, or even unattainable for the majority. In the modern scientific world, the longest human life on record is the 122 years and 164 days of Jeanne Calment, who died in 1997.[8]

Yet in fiction, legend, mythology and, of course the *Bible*, we find propositions for much longer lives. In romantic literature, longevity has been portrayed as a uniquely distinguishing feature. Gagool, in Henry Rider Haggard's *King Solomon's Mines*, is the centenarian witch doctor who guards the secret to a legendary treasure; Haggard's *She*, introduces the immortal queen Ayesha, who must be obeyed.[9] For more recent examples we need look no further than J.K. Rowling's *Harry Potter* series, and the number of distinguished senior wizards who commonly live to be several hundred years old. Many science fiction writers, such as Arthur C. Clark, have taken a more prophetic view, seeing longevity as a miracle of futuristic medicine or science. For Americans today, longevity is no longer a matter of science fiction; it is a startling reality. According to the U.S. Census Bureau, by the year 2100, the United States will have some 5.3 million inhabitants aged over 100.[10]

How do we measure the aging of America? For a start, we can look at life expectancy — the average expected remaining lifetime of each individual in a particular demographic group. Usually life expectancy is stated at birth; although, as we shall soon see, in most developed countries your life expectancy actually *increases* as you get older.

Changes in Life Expectancy

Average life expectancy in the United States today stands at a record 77.6 years, compared to only 47.3 years at the beginning of the 20th century.[11] But remember, this figure is somewhat misleading as it only represents your average life expectancy at birth. A more realistic approach is to look at what we call *age-adjusted* life expectancy, the projection of how long you can be expected to live based on your current age. Age-adjusted life expectancy takes into account not only the important factor of infant mortality, but also the quality of healthcare you may expect to receive in your senior years. For example, a person born in 1980 had a life expectancy at birth of 73.7 years. If that person retires in 2045 at age 65, he or she may then expect to live for a total of 81.4 years. Upon reaching age 75, that same person can look forward to a further 10.4 years of hopefully happy and healthy life to the ripe old age of 85.4.[12] Indeed, the likelihood that an American who makes it to age 65 will survive to age 90 has almost doubled since 1960 to 25 percent.[13] Your chances of spending at least 25 years in retirement are about one in four and growing.

The dramatic increase in our life expectancy over the last century is largely the result of significant improvements in public health, medicine and nutrition. For example, a hundred years ago, lower levels of life expectancy, even in developed countries, were due to extremely high infant and child mortality rates. Advances in medicine and public health have increased the numbers of people living beyond childhood into middle and old age. Samuel Preston, Frederick J. Warren Professor of Demography at the University of Pennsylvania and Director of its Population Studies Center, attributes the most significant gains in life expectancy during the twentieth century to rapid improvements in preventative medicine, the so-called "germ theory" of medicine, and its profound impact on reducing mortality in the developed world, particularly infant mortality. But he also notes that, since the 1960s, the changes have been more the result of advances in big medicine: "The spread of drugs to control high blood pressure is certainly part of the story. So may be advances in cardiovascular surgery and in the emergency treatment of heart attacks."[14]

How Long Can You Live?

The U.S. Census Bureau forecasts that average American life expectancy will be in the mid-80s by the year 2050 and then peak somewhere in the low 90s,[15] unless advances in medical science alter or even reverse the effects of aging as opposed to simply treating them. While historically most increases in life expectancy have been the result of preventing early deaths, experts now predict that the future emphasis will be on the reversal of aging and its effects. In the developed world, for example, recent increases in obesity rates, particularly among the relatively young, led to speculation over *reduced* potential for longer life, due to rises in cancers, heart disease and diabetes. Professor Jay Olshansky of the University of Illinois stated that "… within the next 50 years, life expectancy at birth will decline, and it will decline as a result of the obesity epidemic that will creep through all ages like a human tsunami." Today, more than 30 percent of Americans — almost 59 million people — are classified as obese. Obesity triples the risk of heart disease and produces a tenfold increase in the likelihood of diabetes.[16] However, we should also note that advances in medical science continue to slash the death rates. In 2003, the heart disease death rate decreased to 232.1 per 100,000 from 240.8 in 2002; the cancer death rate fell from 193.5 to 189.3 per 100,000; stroke deaths declined by some 4.6 percent; chronic respiratory diseases by 0.7 percent; and flu and pneumonia by 3.1 percent.[17]

HMOs Are Stealing Market Share From Funeral Parlors

Let there be one huge caveat to this apparently good news: Medical treatment is the most expensive cost-of-living factor. We may all live longer, but the cost will be substantial. According to a recent study by the Rand Corporation, if Americans continue to get fatter at current rates, by 2020 about one in every five healthcare dollars spent on people aged 50 to 69 could be the result of obesity.[18] Gradually we start to see a changing picture of elderly America, one full

> *"There is no fixed life span ... no wall of death dictated by basic biology that we are edging toward."[20]*
> — Dr. James Vaupel, Director of the Laboratory of Survival and Longevity, The Max Planck Institute for Demographic Research, Rostock, Germany

of ailing older people with treatable conditions, but with the costs of treatment spiraling. Dr. Leroy Hood, President and Director of the Institute for Systems Biology in Seattle, Washington, believes that life expectancy will increase by as much as 10 or even 20 years by 2035 as the result of advances in DNA sequencing and nanotechnology.[19] Other experts have even speculated that scientific advances may further stretch our life expectancy, effectively rendering us, like Haggard's Ayesha, immortal. Fantastic though that may seem, the factors that have reduced mortality throughout the twentieth century will continue to work throughout the twenty-first. Even with the unlikely scenario of no further advances in disease treatments, there is still tremendous potential for mortality risk reduction, especially in personal health behavior. We are already beginning to see how adopting healthier lifestyles can be facilitated by improvements in education, particularly through doctor's offices and HMOs.

Retiring Earlier

During the last 60 years, America has seen an increasing trend of workers retiring younger. As recently as World War II, the average retirement age was 70. Today it's 62.[21] But taxes are making it more difficult for Americans to accumulate the money they need for this longer retirement. Currently, employees are leaving the workforce at the earliest affordable opportunity, although not always for the best reasons. According to Dallas Salisbury of the Employee Benefit Research Institute,

45 percent of Americans retire sooner than they had planned — half of those because of illness or disability. But how will that early separation impact their retirement plans as their future appears longer and more expensive? Consider this: Over 70 percent of Baby Boomers say they plan to work in retirement.[22] They must have a good reason. The trend to ever-earlier retirement seems to be leveling off in the United States. Here's why.

There's a Chance Your Money Won't Last

What happens if we take the concept of age-adjusted, or a constantly increasing, life expectancy just one step further when looking at the likelihood of outliving your retirement savings? For years, financial planners have used life expectancy as a measure for their clients' planning horizons, and we have already seen how life expectancy has increased. Now let's take another step and consider your likelihood of surviving to a certain age. Ask yourself, what is the probability that at least one member of a 65-year-old couple will survive to at least age 95?

The answer is 30.2 percent.[23] This is perhaps a far more telling, and worrying, statistic than that couple's average life expectancy. "Longevity risk" is the risk that you or your spouse or partner will outlive your retirement assets. In the table below, of those who reach age 65, more than half of single females and more than 40 percent of single males will live to age 85. If these people plan for retirement income only until their life expectancy of 85, they may run out of money before they die.

Chances of a 65-Year-Old Living

The Social Security Administration has also been alarmingly short in its projections for the average length of retirement it may be expected to help fund (whether it has the coffers or not). Its intermediate projection of 80.5 years life expectancy in 2065 is only one year more than the current life expectancy in Japan. This factor serves to underline the many reasons we have to fear that Social

To Age:	Single Female	Single Male	At Least One Member of a Couple
70	94%	92%	99%
75	84%	80%	97%
80	71%	63%	89%
85	53%	41%	72%
90	32%	20%	45%
95	13%	6%	18%

Source: Society of Actuaries

Security benefits will all but cease to exist in the not-too-distant future. It is also one of the driving forces behind speculation that the ages for early and normal retirement (for the purpose of receiving Social Security benefits) will need to be raised proportionally to match projected increases in life expectancy. It is a sad irony. Social Security was established to insure people against the risk of living too long. Now, the greatest threat to the system is that too many will.

America's financial planners are now fully aware, and they are trying their best to inform you, their clients, that you will probably have to stretch your retirement savings over a longer time period than you thought. Worse than that, you're probably not saving enough in the first place. But if your retirement savings and Social Security aren't sufficient to fund a lengthy retirement, what alternatives do you have?

The Third Age: Myth vs. Reality

Have you ever tried to form a mental picture of your retirement? The chances are you have, although you have probably not been totally persuaded by all the television commercials and brochures that show energetic, white-haired couples, strolling arm-in-arm along a beach at sunset. For most Americans, retirement will be anything but an endless vacation. But what will it be?

The Myth

Will your retirement be an active phase of life that includes volunteer work, public service, and continued employment? An AARP survey, conducted in 2003, concluded that many Americans between the ages of 50 and 70 plan to work during what would normally be considered retirement. Forty-five percent of pre-retirees expect to continue working into their 70s or later. And 18 percent of these said they would work until they were 80 or older, or for as long as they were able.[24] The "third age" is a new life stage occurring between middle age and old age. It is the phase where we start to shift our focus from our careers and the welfare of our children to embark on new careers, reinvent ourselves, form new relationships and even develop new ways of relating to our loved ones.

Indeed for some, the third age seems to have no projected end: Recently, the *Los Angeles Times* reported the case of an 81-year-old Minnesota schoolteacher who retired after 60 years' work, only to return to the classroom for the following school year as a substitute teacher. Or in Wyoming, the 93-year-old surveyor who pounds his own stakes — full time. According to the Labor Department, the number of employed workers 75 and older grew from 669,000 in 1994 to just under 1 million in 2004. It is tempting to assume that the aging of the Baby Boomers will increase these numbers.[25]

The coming of the third age may well be one of the most important stories of our time, but not necessarily for the reasons many commentators think. Let's take a closer look at this phenomenon: In that 2003 AARP survey, 68 percent of those between the ages of 50 and 70 said they expected to work past normal retirement age. But the number one reason given was financial need.[26] And even then, a large portion of these people will be making an erroneous, and perhaps dangerous, assumption.

Reality

Americans are suffering a common misperception that they will select their own schedule for retirement. In fact, many of them point out that they are fortunate enough to enjoy their work and that they will simply keep working. But the reality is that two out of every five Americans won't have a choice of when they retire, because of health issues or job changes.

Let's first take a look at health: There is another common misperception that we will live long, healthy lives, and then finally pass away at the speed of flipping a light switch. Unfortunately the facts say otherwise.

Already some 30 percent of the nation's Medicare budget is spent on the participants' last year of life, often for time spent in the hospital, urgent care, or a skilled nursing unit. This is usually time spent recovering, but seldom totally recovering, from a debilitating event such as a fall, pneumonia, heart attack or a stroke. It may be time spent in weakness, fear, confusion and frustration; time spent waiting to be moved to a longer-term care facility. The reality is that one out of every four of us may possibly spend at least 18 months in long-term care at an average cost of more than $70,000 per year. What few people realize is that there is no Medicare coverage for long-term custodial nursing home care.

Probably the greatest dent to the lifestyles of future retirees will come from the costs of long-term care insurance and nursing home fees. Since the 1990s, many employers have been cutting off medical insurance for retirees, while others don't have any programs at all. This is compounded by the fact that HMOs are charging retirees ever-increasing premiums for medical coverage.

Older Workers = Lower Pay

The employment landscape is by no means certain either. Never mind the golf course, a large portion of us will be lucky if we can decide how much of our retirement we spend at the office, not to mention how much money we earn in the process. Postponed retirement has become a recurring feature of U.S. legislation. In 1978, it became illegal to force a worker into retirement before age 70. In 1986, compulsory retirement was abolished. Companies are obliged to demonstrate that their senior workers can no longer perform their duties before axing them. In 2000, the traditional age of retirement with full Social Security benefits, then 65, began to creep higher. It is currently on track to hit 67 by the year 2022 because Social Security coffers will last longer if retirees either collect no benefits at all for two more years, or retire at the age of 65 on less than full benefits. However, as a money saving tactic, a series of two-year delays is unlikely to keep pace with projected increases in life expectancy. We should continue to expect the future value of Social Security benefits to decline, while the taxes on them rise. So the answer may indeed be to work longer, if we can. But working longer is going to be anything but a breeze. Current economic reality forces us to acknowledge that older workers may have to accept lower pay if they are to remain employed.

If you work for a large company that wishes to remain competitive in a global market, don't expect to keep the same job for the same pay after you retire. All corporations are anxious to cut costs, and current global trends, including outsourcing and the layoff of highly paid senior workers, fuel cost cutting. But all is not lost. Both the Internal Revenue Service and the U.S. Treasury Department are looking at rules, scheduled for 2006, for phased retirement designed to enable older workers to keep working after retirement while their employers reduce their hours. These workers would receive a prorated portion of their pay and, if applicable, of their corporate pension.

For some larger companies it may even be possible to restructure their workforces to take advantage of the healthcare benefit savings brought by the supply of older workers. These older employees are not only experienced, they are eligible for Medicare and will have fewer dependents, making them less expensive in terms of healthcare benefits.[28] In fact, companies may increasingly hire older workers due to shortages in skilled and experienced labor.

But all this does not necessarily mean that corporate employers will provide enough permanent jobs for postponed-retirement workers. Some retirees may return to work for their former employers as consultants. There could well be a surge in start-up home businesses and, for many pre-retirees, the solution must be self-employment.

The most likely trend to emerge from these factors is that of retirement in stages. We know that benefits are no longer improving, and that today's service economy offers more of the kind of jobs older workers are likely to take. Joseph Quinn of Boston College has estimated that already about half of all Americans retire in stages, taking what he calls "bridge" jobs on the way. These jobs are often part-time or self-employed.

Slaying the Retirement Dream

If you are a Baby Boomer, you most likely grew up with icons: James Dean, Buddy Holly, Marilyn Monroe, Elvis ... whose "live fast and die young" creed signified your generation, whether you believed in it or not. The Boomers were not supposed to live until age 85. But they are, and they may not be able to spend all of their golden years playing. Some adjustments are going to be necessary.

Most pre-retirees are starting to realize the truth about how they will fare in retirement. The 2004 Employee Benefits Research Institute's (EBRI) Retirement Confidence Survey found that 24 percent of pre-retirees thought they would live well in retirement and 26 percent believed they would have enough money to cover basic needs. But only 23 percent thought they would not outlive their money. This highlights a common brand of dangerous optimism. The EBRI also found that 30 percent of 45- to 54-year-olds, and 29 percent of those 55 and older, had less than $25,000 in savings and investments. Only 10 percent of the 45- to 54-year-olds, and 13 percent of those 55 and up had $250,000 or more. Financial advisors across the country are faced with the challenge of telling their clients that they cannot expect to make double-digit percentage withdrawals from their portfolios. This reality check is hard for many Baby Boomers to take, especially those who optimistically assume their money will always earn at least 10 percent a year and that they can take out six or seven percent in income annually. A more feasible withdrawal from assets is about four percent a year. When you plug in the idea that most people will need 70 percent to 80 percent of their pre-retirement income during their retirement years, you start to see that a $1 million or even $2 million nest egg just won't be enough. You may have to postpone that move to a golf community. Instead, you may find yourself having to retire where the work is.

Can it get any worse? Absolutely. Let's assume that you have done your homework, you have a plan, and you have made what you hope is the right asset allocation for your long-term financial goals. These preparations could all be torpedoed by the high and very unpredictable cost of healthcare for your long life. Increasingly we find medical professionals telling us that even some modest lifestyle changes in middle age and later can significantly improve our health and longevity. It is recommended that we eat more green, leafy vegetables, perform simple exercises and consume more vitamins B12 and D.[30] It will pay to listen to this advice, not just in years lived, but in the cost of health during those years.

What sort of lifestyle adjustments might become necessary in a typical Baby Boomer's retirement? It may mean municipal golf courses … a used Honda instead of a brand-new Lexus … giving up on that triple non-fat decaf frappuccino … the CD instead of the live concert

The AARP estimates that 46 percent of people over 65 will live in nursing homes for some time during the next 20 years, costing as much as $100,000 per year. This is a devastating drain on resources for many retirees.[29]

… expanding the home cooking repertoire. And in our later years, it may mean something else: perhaps not being able to get out of bed unaided, let alone being able to swing a golf club. Retirement may mean a lot of things, and they will certainly all add up in cost. Most of all, a long life may not mean what you thought it meant.

Harold and Edna Hall – Thirty Years in Retirement

Meet the Halls, Harold and Edna. Harold is 94; Edna is 85. They have been married for 60 years. They have lived in the same house for 53 years. Their daughter Diane is 55 years old. Harold has been retired from his position with the Detroit Symphony Orchestra for 28 years — and counting. The Halls are a living example of people who have spent almost as many years in retirement as they spent working.

The stage for Harold and Edna's life together was set years earlier during the 1920s. Harold was a talented musician who played the violin and oboe, and was encouraged to perform by friends and family. Harold's carefree youth, like the lives of so many others, was interrupted by the Great Depression of the '30s, as his parents faced unemployment and economic insecurity.

However, even in the middle of the Depression, Harold's musical talent merited a full scholarship to the University of Miami in Florida. He and his fellow music students studied hard in school and practiced their survival skills at the same time. "My friends and I were the nucleus of the music department there. Fourteen of us got together and rented a little house."

"In those days, the government's WPA [Works Progress Administration] came through with something like $15 a month for food for each of us students. We all pooled our money for food and rent. The rent was only $15 a month. And by the end of the year, we had enough left over to give each guy about eight bucks apiece to get home on."

After graduation, Harold headed back to Detroit where he joined a WPA symphony formed by the government to support unemployed musicians. "Later I auditioned for a job with the real Detroit Symphony Orchestra. In a few weeks the manager came to me and said, 'Victor Kolar [the DSO's music director and conductor] likes your playing, you've got the job.' So this was on a Sunday in 1942. But within the week after I got the job, I got my draft notice as World War II was underway."

When Harold Met Edna

The war ended and Harold returned to civilian life in the States. As Edna describes it, "Harold was back from the war. He was over 30 and his family was saying, 'Oh, Harold, the old bachelor.' But my friend June, who knew Harold, played matchmaker and introduced us." Harold adds, "June said 'I've got just the girl for you,' and I said, 'Here we go again.'" When Harold and Edna met, they hit it off right away. "She was a beautiful redhead then," says Harold. "After about three days, I had my mind made up."

Harold rejoined the Detroit Symphony Orchestra, performing and traveling throughout Michigan, America and the world. He played oboe and English horn, and he also had duties as an equipment manager. This was an important position, especially when you consider that some of the orchestra's instruments, such as the violins, could cost $1 million a piece!

Harold retired in 1977 at the then-compulsory age of 65. He had a $400 a month pension. "It's at $800 now," he points out. "It's doubled."

Longevity in Retirement

The Halls manage their retirement as they have managed their entire lives: They live within their means. "I've had a rule ever since I bought my first car, when I took out a loan," says Harold. "After a few payments, I couldn't stand it. So I got enough money together to pay it off, and we haven't had anything except the house on payments since then. We have credit cards, but we pay them off every month."

Together with their pension, the Halls collect Social Security. They have made ends meet in other ways, giving music lessons in their home-built studio. Fortunately, they have also been active investors. Not being experts, they did it by pooling their resources, not unlike Harold's student days. "Every month, we'd throw in ten bucks apiece and buy some kind of stock, and the account would build up. And through the years it turned into a pretty good investment."

The Halls have advice for those who are seeking a long life and a successful retirement, "I don't smoke, and I don't make a sport of eating," he says. "Don't just sit around either. A doctor friend of mine told me the life expectancy of typical workers after they retire and sit down and drink beer and watch television is not very long."

Edna adds, "I think people should start planning before retirement, picking what they would like to do more than anything else and go for that goal. Plan for it. It's amazing to see the number of people who return to work after they retire and get a job just for something to do."

Harold and Edna Hall saved and sacrificed. They built their nest egg and followed their plans through to a comfortable retirement. And it's fortunate that they did, because, true to the predictions of the Aging America, they have spent almost as many years in retirement as they spent in the workforce.

Harold and Edna sum it all up by saying, "It's been a good life."

[1] National Vital Statistics Report, 2003.
[2] Raoul Lowery Contreras, "The Rise of Un-American Know-Nothings," *CalNews.com,* March 23, 2000.
[3] "Beyond 50: A Report to the Nation on Economic Security," EBRI, 2004.
[4] Experience Corps, Fact Sheet on Aging in America, *www.experiencecorps.org.*
[5] Steven Reinberg, "Hypertension Undertreated in Elderly," *HealthDay News,* July 27, 2005.
[6] U.S. Census Bureau.
[7] Don Kuhn, "Part II: Shopping for Long Term Care Insurance" (April 2003).
[8] The Guinness Book of Records.
[9] Henry Rider Haggard, "She," Dell Mapback No. 339, New York, 1949.
[10] "America in 100 Years," National Center For Policy Analysis, 2006.
[11] Jay Palmer, "Live to 150," *Barron's,* April 17, 2006.
[12] Centers for Disease Control and Prevention, National Vital Statistics Reports, 2005.
[13] Ibid.
[14] Experience Corps, Fact Sheet on Aging in America, *www.experiencecorps.org,* 2002.
[15] Rachel Zimmerman, "Obesity May Shrink U.S. Lifespan," *Wall Street Journal,* March 17, 2005.
[16] Samaul H. Preston, "American Longevity: Past, Present, and Future," Policy Brief No. 7, Syracuse University: 1996.
[17] "Trimming U.S. Life Expectancy," *Newsday,* February 4, 2005.
[18] "Death Rate From Obesity Gains Fast on Smoking," *Reuters,* March 10, 2004.
[19] "Trimming U.S. Life Expectancy," *Newsday,* February 4, 2005.
[20] Gina Kolata, "Could We Live Forever?" *The New York Times,* November 11, 2003.
[21] "Beyond 50: A Report to the Nation on Economic Security." AARP, 2002.
[22] U.S. Bureau of Labor Statistics study, quoted on Employee Benefit Research Institute (EBRI) web site. http://www.ebri.org/publications/facts/index.cfm?fa=0701fact.
[23] Study by Merrill Lynch, cited by Ellen Uzelac, author of "What a Long, Strange Trip It'll Be," *Research Magazine* (May 2005).
[24] The Annuity 2000 Table.
[25] S. Kathi Brown, Staying Ahead of the Curve 2003: The AARP Working in Retirement Study, Washington, DC: *AARP,* 2003.
[26] Catherine Saillant, "A New Wrinkle in the Workforce," *Los Angeles Times,* February 24, 2005.
[27] Ibid.
[28] Jim Jubak, "What if Nobody Retires?" *MSN Money,* 2005.
[29] Ibid.
[30] "Don't Go Yet," *Economist.com,* March 25, 2004.

*More than 1,000 employers voluntarily shut down
their defined benefit pension plans every year,
leaving a shrinking pool of employers paying into
the federal retirement insurance program that funds
the pensions of bankrupt companies.*

Chapter Two ◀
The Pension Plunge

Retirement is often viewed as a three-legged stool with personal savings, a defined benefit pension plan, and Social Security as the three supporting legs. To most observers, retirement was considered secure — something a worker could look forward to, and count on when retirement arrived. Parents of Boomers have, for the most part, flourished in retirement. They have enjoyed solid pension income streams, supported by Social Security benefits and pockets of personal savings hidden away for special needs. Boomers' parents have enjoyed leisure time, travel and worry-free living; their experience has become the ideal that American workers look to emulate.

Today, the notion of the retirement ideal has fallen on hard times; the stool is increasingly supported by legs in danger of collapse. Pensions are in decline, Social Security faces an uncertain future and American workers aren't putting away much in the way of savings. In fact, given the increase in longevity discussed in the previous chapter, retiring Boomers may run out of income during retirement. Rather than enjoying leisure time, travel and worry-free living, Boomers may spend retirement worrying about how to meet basic living expenses and pay for health care. Retirees may be forced to return to work to supplement their meager retirement incomes. Such a contrast raises the obvious question — how did this shift happen? Increased longevity is only one reason. Legacy costs and the lack of personal savings must also be considered.

Emergence of Legacy Costs

American workers and American industry have operated under an implicit arrangement for at least the last half of the 20th century — workers provided hard labor and companies provided compensation for the worker. Most of the salary came in the form of an immediate paycheck. However, after World War II, many American companies, in an effort to retain cash needed for company operations, started offering workers deferred compensation in return for lower wage increases.[1]

The deferred compensation held out promise for the American worker. It was like a part of the American dream, a promise made by companies to their employees: "For your decades of toil, you will be assured of retirement benefits like a pension and health care."[2] Assets were put aside, then invested by employers and returned in the future as pension payments. Workers essentially gave up immediate income for the promise of more comfort in retirement. Thus, workers waited for this income so they could have a comfortable standard of living in their old age.[3] Pension payments gave rise to part of what has come to be known as a company's legacy costs. The other part is health care benefits, discussed in a later chapter.

Workers came to rely on a company's promises, even to the point of planning their retirement based on the promised income from the company. And companies continued to make promises of deferred compensation without much thought to the debt being accumulated. It wasn't until the late 1980s and early 1990s that companies' eyes were opened to the true expense of their legacy costs. The Financial Accounting Standards Board (FASB) made companies start measuring their retiree liabilities and start carrying these liabilities on their books.[4] But during the dot.com boom of the 1990s, rising stock returns fueled the belief that any pension promise could be fulfilled. Union leaders kept asking for higher benefits and employers gladly accommodated them while, at the same time, they were underfunding their commitments.[5] As for union leaders, it didn't matter to them how high the benefits went since they were federally insured.[6]

It has become apparent that legacy costs are crippling the ability of companies to compete in their markets. It started in the 1980s "with the elimination of middle-class, entry-level jobs in lower-paying industries — apparel, textiles and shoes, among others." Now it is spreading to "jobs that pay solid middle-class wages, starting with the steel industry, then airlines and now autos — with no end in sight." Companies are walking away from their promises, "leaving millions of Americans at risk of an impoverished retirement."[7] General Motors Corporation (GM) announced in the fall of 2005 a plan to cut 30,000 jobs, close nine plants and three service and parts operations by 2008 in an effort to save $7 billion. To blame: high labor, pension, health-care and materials costs as well as sagging demand for the sports-utility vehicles and bloated plant capacity.[8]

Even companies whose pension programs appear to be healthy are beginning to shy away from additional increases in legacy costs. For example, in early December 2005, Verizon — America's second-largest telephone company — announced a freeze on the guaranteed pension plan covering its 50,000 managers, and expanded its 401(k) plans instead. Workers will receive the benefits they've already earned, but no new benefits will accrue. Health-care benefits for managers will also take a hit. Why? — To save $3 billion over the next decade, keeping Verizon competitive with rival cable and technology companies that pay lower wages and provide fewer benefits.[9] Today in the private sector, 42.4 percent of workers age 51 or older aren't being offered any type of pension plan at work.[10]

Defined Benefit Plans (the Traditional Pension)

For decades, the traditional pension was *the* retirement plan for most workers. During a worker's years of employment, the company contributed a specified amount of money to a pool of professionally managed assets for the worker. Upon retirement, the pension plan generated a guaranteed monthly income, based on the worker's years of service and income level, which lasted until the worker died.[11] This carefully crafted social contract between industry and labor once represented a dependable revenue stream for retirees, but it is increasingly falling into disrepair and deficit.[12] This is exactly what Alfred P. Sloan, president of General Motors in the 1940s, feared — pensions would become "extravagant beyond measure." But he gave them to the United Auto Workers anyway.[13]

Three factors have been essentially responsible for the demise of defined benefit pension plans: the Great Bear market, the demographic trend toward increased longevity and companies under-funding their own pension plans. First, the collapse of the stock market bubble followed by the Great Bear revealed billion dollar holes in traditional pension plans. Loss in stock value certainly aided this discovery, which was also caused by poor management, poor accounting oversight and company managers who were more concerned with showing a profit than with appropriately funding the pension plan.[14] In fact, at the end of 2001, the off-balance-sheet pension liabilities for the S&P 500 Index companies totaled more than $1 trillion.[15] If you jump ahead to 2005, the market's year-to-date gain for the S&P 500 is only 1.57 percent — far away from the predicted pension return of 8.27 percent for 2005. It now appears that S&P 500 companies may need to add another $40 billion to $50 billion to their pensions as a result of the lower rate of return.[16] In fact, Standard & Poor's estimates that S&P 500 pension plans are under-funded by some 12 percent, or $150 billion.[17]

Second, retirees are living longer; more of them will spend more time in retirement. The simple fact is that the burden of paying for pensions falls mostly on current workers. Until recently, that had not been a problem since the economy and its workforce were larger than the number of elderly in retirement. However, those numbers are changing with a vengeance. The number of retirees receiving pensions is now growing faster than the number of workers contributing to defined benefit plans.[18] Basic reform in traditional pension plans will be unsuccessful until this unfavorable ratio of workers to retirees is addressed.

At some point, young workers are likely to resent having their wages reduced to support pension payments to their Boomer parents and their grandparents. But continued pension payments, in addition to other retirement benefits, will have to be supported either by a company's workers or by taxpayers.[19]

Finally, companies have simply short-changed their workers and retirees by under-funding their pension plans. Over 50 percent of the 100 biggest corporate defined benefit pensions were under-funded to some degree in 2002; 25 percent were less than 90 percent funded. Between 1995 and 2002, flexible funding rules permitted by the government, along with accounting credits, meant that each year during this period no cash contributions were made to an average of 62.5 percent of these pensions.[20]

According to Credit Suisse First Boston (CSFB), approximately 75 percent of the companies in America's S&P 500 had defined benefit plans with total liabilities of $1.4 trillion at the end of 2004. These plans were under-funded by 13 percent, or some $165 billion. And that deficit doesn't include federal, state and local government defined benefit pension plans.[21] Out of the 365 Index members with defined benefit plans, 311 left those plans under-funded in 2004. And a study of these companies' 10K footnotes shows that even the 20 largest contributors to their pension funds in 2004 still need another seven years at current contribution levels to eliminate their plans' unfunded deficits.

How did these companies get in such a mess? Aside from simply not funding at appropriate levels, employers looked at pensions as future liabilities — something that was not of an immediate concern. Consequently, companies figured their present obligation by discounting their future commitments. If interest rates are low, then larger amounts must be set aside, and if interest rates are high, smaller amounts are set aside to fund the plans. What companies have been doing is using the highest rates allowable, which reduces their present funding requirements.[22] The less a company contributes now, the more it must put into the pension fund later. But by that time, sufficient funds may not be available.

Consider the case of GM. The automaker is laboring under a huge existing pension and healthcare burden. Some industry observers believe that GM may soon be forced into Chapter 11 bankruptcy.[23] GM spent over $5 billion on healthcare alone in 2005, an increase of $1 billion dollars over 2004. This adds up to about $1,500 for each car GM makes — about 3 percent of the company's revenues. The U.S. government contends that GM's pension obligations are under-funded by $31 billion. When you add "other post-employment benefits" (OPEBs) — which consist mainly of retiree health benefits — GM's unfunded liability is estimated at $70 billion. And this deficit doesn't include the potential liability of $5 billion to $11 billion in pension payments to former employees as a result of Delphi's — the nation's largest auto parts manufacturer — Chapter 11 filing. Interestingly, GM's stock market capitalization in 2005 was only $15 billion.[24]

In early 2006, Delphi asked a bankruptcy judge to void its union contracts and let it slash workers' pay, in some cases, by as much as 25 percent. Voiding the labor contracts would also rid Delphi of the pensions and retiree health benefits that it currently carries. For GM, this would mean that it would ultimately be responsible for Delphi's pensions and retiree benefits

"There's no business in America that isn't going to figure out a way to get rid of [these benefit promises]"
— Elizabeth Warren, Law Professor, Harvard University

because of the agreement made when GM sold its parts business to Delphi. As noted above, this obligation is between $5 billion and $11 billion — not what GM needed at the same time it was trying to offer buyouts to its employees to avoid its own pension and retiree health obligations. But that's not the worst scenario.

The United Auto Workers (UAW) threatened to strike Delphi if future labor negotiations did not give UAW employees what they wanted from the company. A strike would cripple the entire U.S. auto industry, but it would hit GM the hardest. GM gets most of its auto parts, about $13 billion worth, from Delphi. Estimates put GM's losses during the first two months of a strike at $8 billion. If the strike were prolonged, GM would have to close its doors because it could not get enough parts from other suppliers to maintain production of its autos. Without cars and without sales, GM would face certain bankruptcy. About the only thing good coming out of such a situation would be the chance for GM to shed its pension and retiree health obligations, and to restructure itself into a smaller, more efficient company. But workers would be left without a viable pension and without healthcare benefits in retirement. For these workers, retirement would clearly be far from the ideal retirement.

In less than ten years, America's steel, airline and, now, auto industries have faced massive legacy costs resulting from past promises made to workers. Several companies — Bethlehem Steel, US Airways, United Airlines, Delta, Northwest and Delphi — have declared Chapter 11 bankruptcy. Companies that have already emerged from bankruptcy are smaller, leaner and generally less burdened by legacy costs. But the trend toward increasing pension problems continues. Already Wall Street is worried about the telecom industry and its potential legacy costs burden, which may have liabilities as high as $20 billion.[25]

Regardless of the industry, companies are piling up deficits in their pension funds that will be hard to eliminate. The accompanying table shows that as the pension fund deficits mount, companies are less able to meet their pension obligations. For example, Delphi Corp. has a $4.3 billion pension fund deficit, and only has enough fund assets to pay about 50 percent of its payment obligations. Ethan Kra, chief actuary for Mercer Human Resources Consulting, said: "If you used the same accounting for the operations side [of a corporation] that is used on the pension funds, you would be put in jail."[26]

OPEB obligations are an even bigger problem than pensions. Pensions have about 88.3 percent of their obligations in pension trusts, compared to 21.7 percent of OPEB obligations. Consequently, the OPEB under-funded liability among the S&P 500 companies is significantly larger than under-funded pension obligations. In the 282 S&P 500 companies offering OPEBs that provided usable data, OPEB assets were $82.2 billion and OPEB obligations were at $379 billion. The under-funded balance of $292.2 billion is 95.1 percent higher than the under-funded pension liabilities of this group of companies.[27]

Disappearing Promises (In Billions)

Company	Pension Deficit	% of Pension Covered
Sara Lee Corp.	$1.5	69.8%
Ford Motors	12.3	83.0%
ExxonMobil	11.5	61.0%
LTV Corp.	1.6	52.0%
Delphi Corp.	4.3	50.0%
Bethlehem Steel	3.7	45.0%
United Airlines	11.0	42.0%
General Motors	31.0	?

Source: Donald L. Barlett and James B. Steele, "The Broken Promise," *Time*, October 31, 2005

Public Pensions

Defined benefit pension problems are not limited to corporate America. Federal, state and local municipalities are also hit hard by pension problems. According to the U.S. Census Bureau, major public pension plans paid out $78.5 billion in the 12 months ended September 30, 2000. By comparison, in 2004, that payout increased to $117.8 billion — a 50 percent increase in five years.[28] Overall, about 90 percent of public workers are covered by defined benefit pensions, compared to 20 percent of private workers.[29]

This debt will not go away or slow down. Even if you exclude federal employees, more than 14 million public workers and 6 million public retirees are owed $2.37 trillion by more than 2000 different state, city and governmental agencies. In 2003 alone, some $46.2 billion was poured into these plans — a 19 percent increase over 2002.[30]

Wilshire Associates, an investment advisory company, studied 64 state pension systems and discovered that 54 of them were under-funded by a total of $175.4 billion. Just like corporations, cities and states are staring down the barrel at a charging lion without enough ammunition. For example, in 2005, Philadelphia's police pension fund had only enough assets to cover 59 percent of its promised retirement checks, while Pittsburgh could only cover 33 percent of its police pension obligations. Both cities had recently sold pension-obligation bonds, and yet, they are still this far behind. In Maryland, repairing the teacher's pensions could carry a $480 million price tag. Maryland's teachers in 2005 received pensions equivalent to about 38 percent of their pre-retirement pay compared to a national average of about 57 percent of pre-retirement pay.[31] But perhaps the worst problem belongs to the state of Illinois; its unfunded liability was estimated at $43.1 billion at the end of 2004, twice the size of the state's budget.[32]

It is critical to understand the magnitude of the pension problem since state and local governments have limited financial options. Unlike the federal government, which can print more money, or private companies, which can theoretically sell more products, local government has only one way to fund its promises: taxes. And since most public sector retirement benefits are guaranteed by state constitutions, the obligations cannot be avoided. Several court challenges have produced rulings supporting the notion that benefits promised to public employees must be honored. These liabilities are likely to translate into higher state and local taxes. And unlike private or public companies, local governments cannot declare bankruptcy.

A Tradition in Decline

Bankruptcy is not the only solution to a company's pension obligations. Some companies are freezing the pension benefits for specific workers. When a company freezes its plan, it usually makes the plan unavailable for new employees, and it may stop contributions for workers under a certain age — usually 40. Most employees over 40 are likely to feel threatened by the pension freeze since retirement is fairly close at hand. Freezing is a sure way to increase the complaints and decrease the morale among the older workers.[33]

Freezing is expected to gain momentum as increasing legacy costs become an issue throughout the U.S. economy. In fact, larger employers have accelerated the pace of pension freezes and pension plan terminations, and are shying away from the increasing expenses and uncertainty associated with supporting workers' retirements. In 2004, about 11 percent of large companies offering pension plans terminated or froze benefits, an increase from seven percent in 2003.[34]

The traditional pension system has been in decline for the past 20 years. In recent years, an increasingly large number of companies are shutting down their defined benefit pension plans altogether. Estimates suggest that as many as 1,000 employers voluntarily close their defined benefit plans each year.[35] In 2004, more than 1,200 plans were terminated, and since 2000, over 7,500 plans have been shuttered.[36]

Estimates vary on how many plans are still operating, but the decline is precipitous. In 1985, 114,396 defined benefit plans were active. By 2003, the number dropped to between 31,135 and 29,512 plans. Estimates place the number of plans at 23,000 in 2005.[37]

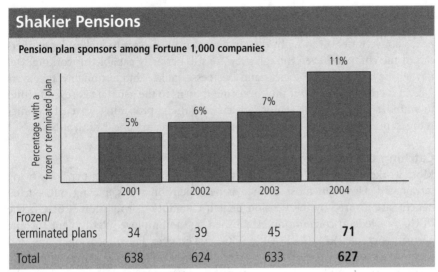

Shakier Pensions

Pension plan sponsors among Fortune 1,000 companies

	2001	2002	2003	2004
Frozen/ terminated plans	34	39	45	**71**
Total	638	624	633	**627**

Source: Watson Wyatt Worldwide

This trend is likely to get worse as fewer companies view retirement as their problem. According to Hewitt Associates, who surveyed 100 large U.S. and European multinational organizations, only four percent said that enabling employees to retire is a top priority. Less than half of the North American organizations ranked themselves as having control over the tools needed for proper retirement planning. In their view, the onus for retirement planning has shifted to the individual.[38]

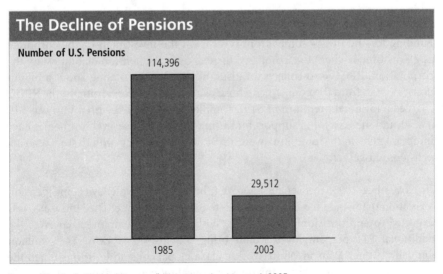

The Decline of Pensions

Number of U.S. Pensions

Source: "The Really Troubled Program," *Time Magazine*, January 4, 2005

If pension plans continue to decline and pension payments decrease, it may force many Boomer retirees to stay in the workforce a lot longer — just to keep their heads above water. Eventually, the tendency for businesses to kick older workers out of the company, even though they are still perfectly capable of working, will have to be addressed by society and businesses alike. Unquestionably, taxpayers face an increasing burden if the government turns to the general tax revenue fund to support pensions. For senior citizens and the approaching wave of Boomer retirees, prospects for a solid retirement income stream appear dim, at best.

Catching the Fallout

Most workers experience high anxiety at the thought of their pensions being terminated. However, most defined benefit pension plans, paying out a fixed benefit, are insured by the Pension Benefit Guaranty Corporation (PBGC). The PBGC is a federal corporation established by the Employee Retirement Income Security Act of 1974 (ERISA).[39] PBGC takes over failed pension plans and administers the plan's benefits to covered employees. The PBGC stands behind the pensions of 44 million Americans, mostly in mature industries such as the airlines, steel and automakers.[40]

Most of the plans taken over by the PBGC come from liquidated companies. The PBGC petitions the bankruptcy court to acquire the pension plans. A company in bankruptcy may request that its pension plan be given to the PBGC because the company couldn't survive if it had to continue making pension plan contributions. If the judge agrees, PBGC must take over the plan, as it did on May 10, 2005, when a bankruptcy judge allowed United Airlines to give up its pension plans. All of a sudden, the PBGC became responsible for $6.6 billion of United's under-funded pensions.[41] PBGC also may initiate a plan takeover on its own by asking the court for the termination of a company's plan.[42]

Funding for the PBGC comes from returns on the investment of the corporate assets assumed when the company turned over its pension liabilities to the corporation. PBGC also collects an insurance premium, totaling about a billion dollars a year, from the companies whose plans it guarantees.[43] Initially, the PBGC charged a minimal premium of $1 per employee. In 2005, the premium was $19 a head, and there's a lot of support for raising the cost. But several companies have indicated that if the premium were to be increased, they would stop offering pensions altogether.[44]

In November 2005, the Senate approved, by a 97 to 2 vote, sweeping pension legislation that would increase premiums to $30 per employee. The House also was expected to approve similar legislation. With 44 million employees covered, the additional $11 per employee would bring the PBGC an extra $484 million annually.[45] When Watson Wyatt Worldwide, a global consulting firm, studied the proposal, it concluded that companies with healthy pension plans could see 240 percent increases in total PBGC premiums compared to 113 percent premium increases for companies with unhealthy pension plans.[46] The Bush administration threatened to veto the legislation because it didn't go far enough. As for companies with pension plans, they may move more quickly to defined contribution plans if the legislation passes. At the end of the first quarter of 2006, the House and Senate were still in negotiation on a comprise bill. The hang-up appeared to be a House provision that would let mutual fund companies advise 401(k) participants about fund selection, which the Senate said was a conflict of interest.

The PBGC may also be able to secure funds from its increasing shareholder status in the airline, and possibly the auto industry. A federal bankruptcy judge gave the PBGC seven percent of US Airways Group shares as compensation for its under-funded plan. The corporation was also granted 24.4 percent of United Airline's new shares, and stands to inherit sizeable chunks of Northwest Airlines, Delta Air Lines and Delphi Corp., if these companies ask the bankruptcy judge to shed their pension plans.[47] Selling this stock after the companies emerge from bankruptcy could help fund future pension payments.

To this point, no taxpayer money has been used to fund the PBGC or pay out any of its assumed pension payments. However, given its mounting deficit problem, most observers doubt that the PBGC will be able to survive without some sort of taxpayer support. PBGC's only other source of funds is a $100 million line of credit from the U.S. Treasury.

PBGC will pay out pension checks until its funds are exhausted, which is projected to occur sometime around 2013. "At that point, Congress will be forced to decide whether to bail out the agency at a cost of $100 billion or more. When judgment day comes, other economic forces will influence the decision."[48] Medicare, Medicaid, Social Security and all other entitlement programs will be fighting for an ever-larger share of the funds that Congress throws in their direction. Given the competition, the PBGC looks to be a pretender rather than a contender.

In 2004, the PBGC had $62.3 billion in long-term obligations to more than 1.1 million people, including over 500,000 current retirees. It had $39 billion in assets; thus, it finished the year with a $23.3 billion deficit.[49] Since then, things have gotten worse. The PBGC has been given United Airlines' $6.6 billion pension fund. Recently, Delta Air Lines and Northwest Airlines filed for Chapter 11 bankruptcy, and if they convince a judge

> *"PBGC's accumulated deficit is too big, and plans simply do not have enough money in the system to back up the long-term promises many employees have made to their workers."*
> — Government Accounting Office

that their pension plans are a threat to their continued survival, the PBGC will acquire an estimated $12.4 billion in new unfunded liabilities.[50] In addition, the pensions at bankrupt Delphi Corp. are under-funded by an estimated $4.3 billion, which, if terminated, would eventually fall to the PBGC.[51] In 2004, the PBGC calculated that financially weak companies with a good chance of terminating their pension plans are about $96 billion short of covering their promises to employees.[52]

The pressure on the PBGC continues to mount, with no apparent source of additional funds to support new pension payments. If nothing is done, the PBGC deficit will surely continue to expand. The Congressional Budget Office recently estimated that the deficit will increase to $86.7 billion by 2015, and to $141.9 billion by 2025.[53] Congress has pledged help for PBGC. Yet, Congress continues to make it easy for those same defaulting companies to avoid making payments to their pension funds, making the funds more susceptible to being taken over by the PBGC.[54] While the government sends mixed signals, the PBGC is left to enlarge both its obligations and its deficit.

In 2005, the PBGC said it was paying full benefits to roughly 90 percent of the participants who now get their checks from a corporation. The other 10 percent are receiving less than promised. In the case of some higher paid participants, such as airline pilots, benefits may be cut by 60 to 70 percent, or more. The accompanying table shows that for the year 2005, full benefits for a 65-year-old retiree were $45,614 (in 2006, this increased to $47,659).[55] But if a worker retires before age 65, benefits decrease substantially. These limits apply regardless of the benefits you were promised. And they are frozen in the year the PBGC assumed responsibility for your pension plan. If the plan terminated in 2005, the workers who retire in 2015 will be stuck with the 2005 limits for their age at retirement.[56] Needless to say, the termination of a corporate pension plan and its transfer to the PBGC has the potential to be devastating to plan participants, especially considering that inflation is not built into future payments.

Pension Benefit Guarantee Corporation
(Pension Benefits Paid 2005)

Age	Monthly Benefit	Annual Benefit
65	$3,801	$45,614
62	$3,003	$36,035
60	$2,472	$29,649
55	$1,712	$20,526

Source: "How Safe Is Your Pension Benefit?" *Kiplinger's Retirement Report* (August 2005)

So Who's Responsible Now?

Companies can sponsor two types of retirement plans: the traditional defined benefit plan, which we have just shown is in decline, or the defined contribution plan, which appears to be on the rise. For years, the predominant plan offered by companies was the defined benefit plan. However, over the past two to three decades there has been a slow, uninterrupted shift from defined benefit plans to defined contribution plans. All the evidence suggests that since 401(k)s were introduced in the early 1980s, companies have been working to shift workers out of pension plans into savings plans. This shifts the emphasis from the pension leg of the stool to the personal savings leg of the stool.

This shift also brings fundamental changes in the allocation of risk, plan responsibility and planning emphasis. For example, defined benefit plans are sponsored by the company, and the company contributes money to the plan for all workers employed by the company. Risk is allocated (shared) across all workers so that no one worker stands to lose or gain as a result of his or her own investment. Employees can come to work and merrily go about their jobs without worrying about their retirement. The plan is managed by someone else, and the company is responsible for providing a monthly retirement paycheck for each worker when he or she reaches retirement.[57]

In most defined contribution plans, companies are not responsible for contributing assets to the plan unless they agree to match the employee's contribution. With 401(k)s, for example, the risk is not shared across all employees. The individual employee decides on the level of plan contribution, if any, how the assets will be allocated, and what part this personal savings will play in his or her overall retirement plan. When a company offers employees a defined contribution plan, it shifts plan responsibility, allocation of risk and the risk of earning insufficient returns to the individual employee.[58]

The bottom line is that individuals are being asked to assume more of the financial responsibility for their future. They are being asked to invest in defined contribution plans, consider private accounts for Social Security, and use health savings accounts. It's the individual's responsibility to keep spending in check, and make sure that adequate contributions are being made to personal accounts to provide a future retirement income stream. The era of the welfare state is increasingly giving way to individual self-sufficiency. More and more Americans are on their own, and responsible for their impending retirement.

What?! Me Save?!

Left to their own devices, most American workers do not save enough for their retirement, if they save at all. Yet, this is what the defined contribution plan does — puts the onus for saving directly on the individual worker. Yes, the defined contribution plan allows employers to help workers build up a nest egg for retirement through tax-deferred contributions, but the employer has few of the expenses and responsibilities incurred in a defined benefit plan. While many employers do match or supplement employee contributions, the real burden is on the worker. If the worker doesn't contribute to the 401(k), there will be little or no retirement income stream from the defined contribution plan during retirement.

Unfortunately, the American worker's — especially the Boomers — track record on saving is rather dismal. For instance, more than half of the nation's 132 million workers do not participate in any kind of employer-provided pension or retirement plan. People in their mid 50s and early 60s had median savings of just $42,000 in retirement accounts in 2001, well below the estimated $1 million that most financial advisers believe the average household with an annual income of $40,000 will need for a comfortable retirement.[59] Surveys of pre-retirees find that as many as 40 percent of them haven't done any planning at all,[60] and nearly 28 million U.S. households — 37 percent of the total — do not own a retirement account of any kind.[61]

Clearly, the American worker's propensity to save is quite small; we have already established that the national personal savings rate for 2005 was -0.5 percent of income.[62] It's a wonder the retirement stool isn't more lopsided, given the shortness of the personal savings leg. If workers are to have any chance at a comfortable retirement, they must be convinced to save more, starting with contributions to employer-sponsored defined contribution plans.

Current Situation

In 2004, more than 42 million Americans had a total of $1.9 trillion invested in 401(k) plans, and almost half of that money was in mutual funds.[63] According to government figures, only 47 percent of private companies offer defined contribution plans, and employee participation by workers age 16 and above is in the 40 to 50 percent range. And it's been that way for the past 25 years. Of workers aged 25 to 64, participation runs between 60 and 65 percent. Over time, deferral rates for employee contributions into these plans has averaged about six percent of pay.[64] However, in 2003, the average employee contribution among workers participating in 401(k)s was 7.5 percent.[65]

But it's probably not reasonable, at this time, to call defined contribution plans an effective substitute for defined benefit plans. If you look behind the nearly $2 trillion in these accounts, there is less to be awed about. In 2004, the media made much of the fact that the value of the average 401(k) account had climbed to $61,000. However, if you look at the median value, the point at which half of all accounts hold less, and half of all accounts hold more, the value was $17,909 in 2004. And nearly 25 percent of these accounts had balances of less than $5,000.[66] This paints an entirely different picture of the health of America's retirement system.

Lack of Participation

In a 2005 study by *The Wall Street Journal Online* and Harris Interactive, one-third of the Americans surveyed expected to have enough money saved to retire comfortably, 39 percent were not sure, and 27 percent didn't think they would have sufficient funds for a comfortable retirement.[67] Yet, many of these same Americans appear not to be participating in defined contribution plans.

About 45 percent of working American adults say they participate in a 401(k) or a 403(b) plan. Thirty-five percent of working adults report that such plans are not available to them, and when they are available, 14 percent of adults simply don't participate.[68] Workers in the lower income brackets are less likely to participate; 22 percent of those with incomes below $35,000 participate, while 66 percent of workers making over $75,000 participate. According to John Bogle, founder of the Vanguard Group, despite having at least a quarter-century to build assets in tax-sheltered, defined contribution plans, workers have made a miserable effort at building their accounts.

If workers are left to decide for themselves about participation, many of them will take no action. Exhortations to save seem to fall on deaf ears, and even generous incentives get ignored. To combat this apathy, the Department of Labor proposed a regulation, at the end of 2005, that would encourage companies to automatically enroll their employees in 401(k) plans. In 2005, only 19 percent of companies automatically enroll workers at an average deferral rate of three percent of income. Automatic enrollment can be effective in boosting participation, especially among younger workers and lower-income workers.[69] The same things that keep workers from enrolling are likely to keep them from dis-enrolling — inconvenience and inaction. In the spring of 2006, Congress was considering a bill that would encourage automatic 401(k) enrollment of employees.

In one American company, switching to automatic enrollment increased the rate of participation in the 401(k) plan — the main retirement savings option — from 49 percent of newly eligible employees to 86 percent. In addition, getting employees to pre-commit a portion of their future pay raises to their pensions is also effective in increasing participation. For one company, it helped raise the average contribution rate from three-and-a-half percent of income to 13.6 percent over a 40-month period.[70]

The Lure of Money

Besides a lack of participation, getting workers to leave their money in the defined contribution plan is another problem. Forty-five percent of workers who participate in a 401(k) plan opt to cash it out after leaving their jobs. They would rather spend the money instead of leaving it in the plan or rolling it into another plan. Workers with lower-account balances are most likely to cash out; 72.5

percent of employees with balances under $10,000 raid their 401(k)s.[71] Unfortunately, these are the employees who can least afford to cash out their defined contribution plans.

Without question, the security of a guaranteed income stream during retirement is evaporating with the decline of defined benefit pension plans. As more companies realize the potential damage of the legacy costs of benefits they have promised employees over past decades, the less inclined they are to continue being the guardians of their employees' retirement. By offering their employees defined contribution plans, companies have passed that responsibility to individual employees. But these employees have yet to get serious about their retirement futures. For now, it would seem that at least two of the legs of the retirement stool are really quite wobbly, and in the process of collapse.

Frederick (Fritz) Meyer — A Change of Flight Plan

Frederick "Fritz" Meyer is 69 years old, and a retired United Airlines pilot. Fritz was studying electrical engineering at the University of Colorado-Boulder, when the flying bug got him and he became a fighter pilot for the U.S. Navy for six years, flying the F-8 Crusader flown by the Navy's "Top Gun" pilots. For the next 32 years, Fritz flew airplanes for United Airlines. When Fritz started with United, he flew on the DC 6/7s. When he retired, he was flying the "wide bodies" — the DC 10 and the Boeing 747 400. As he moved up to bigger airplanes, his salary and benefits package also increased. Retired for the past nine years, Fritz draws a pension from the United Airlines Pilot's pension plan.

Fritz is married to Judy Meyer, who worked as a United Airlines Flight Attendant for 38 years. At age 63, she is now retired and drawing a pension from the United Airlines Flight Attendant's pension plan.

When Fritz started with United, the package was an annuity retirement. "When you retired, the company bought you an annuity and you were no longer attached to the company," explained Fritz. However, in 1985, United convinced the United Airlines Pilot Association that a company-sponsored, defined benefit pension plan would be better for the pilots and the company. At first, pilots got 9 percent of their monthly pay paid toward their pensions by the company. This promise of a guaranteed income for life was very attractive, so pilots had little problem taking lower salary increases in lieu of enhancing their retirement pensions.

When Fritz retired, all was well with his pension, and he looked forward to his retirement. At the time, he was still two years away from collecting Social Security, but that was almost incidental compared to what his pension would pay him. Then in December 2002, United Airlines filed for Chapter 11 bankruptcy and entered bankruptcy court protection.

After filing for bankruptcy, United went to the pilots union four times seeking wage concessions. United told the pilots that they either accept wage cuts or the company would be forced to shut down and close its doors. The threat of no longer having a job was, of course, a powerful incentive to accept a wage cut. In total, the pilots took an approximate wage cut of 50 percent. But their pensions, although under-funded, were still intact — that is, until December of 2004 when United defaulted on its pension payments, and the Pension Benefit Guaranty Corporation (PBGC) petitioned the court to take it over to avoid having to pay a higher amount starting in 2005, according to Fritz. The petition was granted, but United's unions have all filed suit against this move, and the pensions are, for the moment, still in limbo. There is, however, little doubt that the PBGC will assume responsibility for United's pensions.

For Fritz and his wife, Judy, having the PBGC administer United's pension plans means a cut in benefits. Since the PBGC sets limits on the amount it pays in benefits to retirees, people who receive pension benefits higher than the limit will have their monthly benefits cut. And they will lose all of their non-qualified pension benefits.

Fritz will lose $860 a month in payments from the non-qualified portion of his pension. His wife may also have a cut in her pension benefits, so Fritz has his pension, his wife's pension and their Social Security benefits to rely on in retirement. But with the coming benefit cuts, retirement may not be as exciting as planned.

When asked what he would say to people who are relying on their pensions, Fritz adamantly said, "Don't rely on it!" That's why he is currently starting a retirement plan for his stepdaughter. He is contributing $1,500 a year to a plan that won't interfere with any 401(k) she might start and that's outside of any company plan until she gets out of college and starts her own job. That's his answer to what happened to him. Don't assume that what you've been guaranteed is *really* guaranteed.

---

[1] Ellen E. Schultz, "When Pensions Change Hands, Retirees Can Be Lost in Shuffle," *The Wall Street Journal Online*, May 18, 2005.
[2] Donald L. Barlett and James B. Steele, "The Broken Promise," *Time*, October 31, 2005.
[3] Colleen O'Connor and Kelly Yamanouchi, "Pensions' Empty Promise," *DenverPost.com*, August 28, 2005.
[4] Kelly Yamanouchi, "Pensions Lose Luster For Young Workers," *The Denver Post*, 2005.
[5] Roger Lowenstein, "The End of Pensions?" *The New York Times Magazine*, October 30, 2005.
[6] Ibid.
[7] Barlett and Steele, "Promise," op. cit.
[8] "GM to Cut $30,000 Jobs by 2008, Expects $7 Billion in Savings," *The Wall Street Journal Online*, November 21, 2005.
[9] Joseph Schuman, "Verizon Shifts Managers Retirement Plan," The Morning Brief, *The Wall Street Journal Online*, December 6, 2005.

[10] David Wessel, "How Will the U.S. Fill Its Benefits Gap?" *The Wall Street Journal Online*, April 13, 2006.

[11] Jeff D. Opdyke, "With Thousands of Pensions Closing, How Safe Is Yours?" *The Wall Street Journal Online*, September 15, 2004.

[12] Jyoti Thottam, "The Next Scrambled Nest Egg?" *Time*, August 11, 2003.

[13] Lowenstein, op. cit.

[14] "Getting Greyer — and Poorer Too?" *The Economist.com*, May 30, 2005.

[15] G. Bennett Stewart III, "Pensions Roulette: Have You Bet Too Much on Equities?" *Harvard Business Review* (June 2003).

[16] Howard Silverblatt, "Accounting's New Frontier: Pensions," *BusinessWeek Online*, November 15, 2005.

[17] David Wyss, "Business Reins In Its Debt," *BusinessWeek Online*, April 10, 2006.

[18] "S&L Redux," Buttonwood Column, *The Economist.com*, June 21, 2005.

[19] "Which Side Are You On?" Buttonwood Column, *The Economist.com*, October 11, 2005.

[20] "Report Finds Underfunding at Largest U.S. Pensions," *Insurance Newscast*, June 2, 2005.

[21] "Now for the Reckoning," *The Economist.com*, October 13, 2005.

[22] Lowenstein, op. cit.

[23] "Now for the reckoning," *The Economist.com*, October 13, 2005.

[24] "Reckoning," op. cit.

[25] Ibid.

[26] Barlett and Steele, "Promise," op. cit.

[27] Howard Silverblatt, "America's Other Pension Problem," *BusinessWeek Online*, December 19, 2005.

[28] "Sinkhole! How Public Pension Promises Are Draining State and City Budgets," *BusinessWeek Online*, June 13, 2005.

[29] Donald L. Barlett and James B. Steele, "Where Pensions Are Golden," *Time*, October 31, 2005.

[30] "Sinkhole!," op. cit.

[31] John Wagner, "Teacher Pension Plan Faces Hurdle on Costs," *Washingtonpost.com*, December 18, 2005.

[32] Barlett and Steele, "Golden," op. cit.

[33] "Company Pensions Excluding Young Workers," *Financial Advisor Magazine*, July 22, 2005.

[34] Hubert B. Herring, "It's July 2005. Do You Know Where Your Pension Is?" *The New York Times Online*, July 10, 2005.

[35] Gregory Crawford and Vineeta Anand, "The Looming Retirement Disaster," *Pensions & Investments*, April 18, 2005.

[36] Jeff D. Opdyke, op. cit.

[37] "The Fall of Private Pensions," *The Wealth Management Adviser*, June 9, 2005.

[38] Savita Iyer, "Most Companies See Employee Retirement as Not Their Problem," *Investment Advisor.com*, December 20, 2005.

[39] "Basics of the Pension Benefit Guaranty Corporation (PBGC)," Employee Benefit Research Institute (July 2005).

[40] Susan Cornwell, "U.S. Pension Plans May Not Save Insurer Says Analyst," *Insurance News*, August 5, 2005.

[41] Michael Schroeder, "Looking to Keep Pension Agency Solvent, Congress Fears Backlash," *The Wall Street Journal Online*, May 12, 2005.

[42] Ibid.

[43] Ibid.

[44] Mary Williams Walsh, "Whoops! There Goes Another Pension Plan," *The New York Times*, September 19, 2005.

[45] Michael Schroeder, "Pension Measure Passes in Senate, but Hurdles Loom," *The Wall Street Journal Online*, November 17, 2005.

[46] Barlett and Steele, "Promise," op. cit.

[47] Michael Schroeder, "Pension Insurer Holds 23.4% of Newly Issued UAL Shares," *The Wall Street Journal Online*, February 15, 2006.

[48] Barlett and Steele, "Promise," op. cit.

[49] Walsh, op. cit.

[50] Joseph Schuman, "Airline Chapter 11 Filings Reverberate," The Morning Brief, *The Wall Street Journal Online*, September 15, 2005.

[51] "U.S. Estimates Delphi Owes Pension Funds $10.8 Billion," *Insurance News*, October 13, 2005.

[52] Marilyn Adams, "'Broken' Pension System in 'Crying Need' of a Fix," *USA Today*, November 14, 2005.

[53] Walsh, op. cit.

[54] "Promises, ahem," *The Economist.com*, May 12, 2005.

[55] Savita Iyer, "PBGC Releases Pension Benefit Guarantee for 2006 and Retirement Age Table," *Investment Advisor.com*, December 20, 2005.

[56] "How Safe Is Your Pension Benefit?" *Kiplinger's Retirement Report* (August 2005).

[57] David Blitzer, "Retirement: What Price Risk?" *BusinessWeek Online*, March 31, 2005.

[58] "Enough to Live On," *The Economist.com*, March 25, 2004.

[59] Crawford and Anand, op. cit.

[60] "The Looming Retirement Crisis," *On Wall Street* (June 2004).

[61] Dan Ackman, "Retirement Doomsday," *Forbes.com*, May 4, 2005.

[62] "Economy Accelerates in the Third Quarter," Bureau of Economic Analysis, October 28, 2005.

[63] Ken Brown and Christopher Oster, "As Returns Sag, Employers Turn Up Heat on 401(k) Fees," *The Wall Street Journal Online*, September 14, 2004.

[64] Crawford and Anand, op. cit.

[65] Barry B. Burr, "Participation By Workers in Plans Shows Increase," *Investment News.com*, October 10, 2005.

[66] Barlett and Steele, "Promise," op. cit.

[67] "Many Americans Lack Confidence in Ability to Retire Comfortably," *The Wall Street Journal Online*, September 26, 2005.

[68] "Many Americans Lack Confidence in Ability to Retire Comfortably," op. cit.

[69] Kathy Chu, "Rule Would Encourage Automatic 401(k) Enrollment," *USA Today*, August 21, 2005.

[70] "Pensions by Default," *The Economist.com*, August 27, 2005.

[71] David Ellis, "Retirement Blunder: Raiding the 401(k)," *CNNMoney*, July 25, 2005.

The U.S. government owes Social Security $1.7 trillion, and the debt grows by $200 billion a year.

Chapter Three ◀
Social Insecurity

Social Security is another of the retirement stool's collapsible legs; it began sturdy enough, but it now faces potential bankruptcy. Over the years, Americans' perceptions of Social Security have drifted away from the reality of the program. The political rhetoric surrounding Social Security and the outright deception that has served to hide the program's welfare dimensions. In reality, Social Security's future is far from settled. However, Americans believe that the system is more secure than it is, that Social Security benefits are earned entitlements, that Social Security benefits are guaranteed retirement income and that the program is less costly than it really is. Americans seem ready to defend Social Security to the death, but the reality is that the program is headed for insolvency and is creating a fiscal nightmare that is increasingly difficult to remedy.

Perception and Reality

Perception: Social Security was intended to provide for all the old-age income needs of retirees.

Reality: The Social Security program was intended to provide only a basic floor of income for old age, not to replace private savings. Individuals were encouraged to add further income protection from private alternatives, if they so desired. The program's purpose was to protect the elderly against financial calamity.

Over the years, Social Security has developed a fundamental problem. It was originally intended to provide only a supplemental retirement income source for a minority of Americans. Instead it has become the primary retirement income source for a majority of retired Americans. Additionally, Social Security has blossomed into more than just a retirement program. Through the years, other benefits were added that covered widows, disabled workers and children.

Perception: Social Security was always a pay-as-you-go program.

Reality: The original intent was to make Social Security a self-supporting, fully-funded program that operated in accordance with accepted actuarial principles. General tax revenues were not to be used, except for the first few years, in order to pay the benefits of workers who had not contributed much, or anything, to the system. Taxes were to be collected and invested in a trust fund that would pay for current promised benefits. Future benefits were to be paid from the accumulated trust fund assets.

Several supporters of the Act wanted the program to operate on a pay-as-you-go basis, and their first opportunity to make this change came in 1939 when the Act was amended to include spousal, children's and survivor's benefits. The changeover was fully completed in the early 1940s, and Social Security became a pay-as-you-go program.

Reality: In the late 1930s when Social Security started, approximately 42 workers contributed to Social Security for each beneficiary of the program. By 1945, the "dependency ratio" had fallen to 16 contributors to a single beneficiary, and today the ratio is 3.25 to 1. The number of beneficiaries is expected to double between now and 2030, and the ratio of covered workers to beneficiaries will be down to about 2 to 1.[1] Perhaps, if the money had been put into a fund to draw interest when the amount coming in was higher than the amount paid out, Social Security would not be the troublesome program that it is today.

Reality: In 2005, a 12.4 percent tax was levied on the first $90,000 of an employee's FICA (Federal Insurance Contribution Act) wages. In 2006, the wage cap on which payroll taxes are levied increased to $94,200, meaning that 11.3 million workers will pay higher Social Security taxes.[2] Employees making more than $94,200 don't have to pay tax on the amount above $94,200, but that wage cap may also increase given the need to keep Social Security from financial hardship. In all, an estimated 159 million workers will pay Social Security taxes in 2006. Of the 12.4 percent tax, the employee pays 6.2 percent of the tax and the employer pays the other 6.2 percent. Revenue generated by the tax is used by the federal government to pay the current Social Security benefits, which takes approximately two-thirds of the tax revenues. The remaining one-third is used to pay general federal government obligations, and the government replaces those revenues in the trust fund with an IOU. Currently those IOUs run about $200 billion a year.[3]

Perception: Social Security benefits include only what you have paid into the program.

Reality: Social Security was originally formulated to address the high level of unemployment during the depths of the Great Depression. Consequently, the Social Security Act was structured to discourage the elderly from working so that their jobs would be available for younger workers. To accomplish this, the Act included an earnings means test that stopped benefits if a worker earned more than a certain amount of wages, which tended to discourage full-time employment among workers eligible for Social Security.

In addition, the Act also granted benefits to older workers who had paid little or nothing into the program in order to keep them from working, which freed up jobs for younger workers. These workers received benefits that were in excess of what they had paid into the program.[4]

Reality: In reality, Social Security serves two functions: insurance and welfare. As an insurance program, Social Security recipients are paid benefits based solely on how much they have paid into the program. These benefits are paid out regardless of the level of the individual's need. As a welfare program, Social Security recipients are also paid benefits based on their poverty level or their level of need. The benefits are paid out regardless of how much the individual has paid into the program.

As a consequence of this welfare function, some Social Security recipients, especially lower-income workers, will receive far more from Social Security than they have paid into the program. For example, consider Mr. Stockton's illustration. If he lives to be 85, he will receive approximately nine times more in benefits than he paid into Social Security in taxes. Other recipients, such as higher-income workers, may also receive lifetime Social Security benefits that are

Meet the Stocktons

- Retired in 2001
- Worked 40 years as a welder
- Mrs. Stockton – age 65 when retired
- Mr. Stockton – age 65 when he began his Social Security Benefits
- Initial monthly Social Security benefit of $1,715
- Average lifetime annual benefit of $28,102
- FICA contributions of $64,974 during employment
- If he lives to 85, he will receive $590,162 in benefits

Benefits Calculator www.ssa.gov. Figures include 3% increase per year in CPI.
Sources: Average and Marginal Employee Social Security and Medicare (FICA) Tax Rates for Four-Person Families Same Relative Positions in the Income Distribution – Tax Policy Center, www.taxpolicycenter.org.

several times higher than what they paid into the program. Unfortunately for future retirees, benefit cuts may decrease the amount of lifetime benefits that a beneficiary may expect to receive from Social Security.

Consider the following table:

Social Security Taxes Paid vs. Projected Lifetime Benefits		
Income Percentile	Average Lifetime Amount Paid In	Average Total Lifetime Benefit
Lowest 20%	$11,211	$220,235
Second 5th (20-40%)	$30,978	$370,615
Third 5th (40-60%)	$51,441	$523,403
Fourth 5th (60-80%)	$76,513	$601,518
Top 20%	$87,222	$630,424

Assumptions: Uses the mean earnings for each quintile over 37 years (1967-2003) and historical FICA rates and wage caps. This wage history is used to arrive at the initial Social Security Benefit for a 65 year old with an annual COLA adjustment of 3% and a death age of 85. Sources: [1] U.S. Census Bureau, Current Population Survey, Annual Social and Economic Supplements, 2004. [2] Social Security Administration, Historical Social Security Tax Rates, 2004. [3] Social Security Administration, Social Security Benefits Calculator, 2005.

These data present a clear reason why Social Security is going broke: Half of American workers are projected to receive Social Security benefits of 12 to 20 times as much as they contributed. For instance, the bottom 40 percent of wage earners will have lifetime contributions ranging from $11,000 to $31,000, while drawing lifetime benefits of $220,000 to $370,000. Even the top 20 percent of wage earners may get back over seven times as much as they paid in. Given these ratios, continued solvency for Social Security appears to be an illusion.

Perception: Social Security taxes go directly into "investments" in the Social Security Trust Fund Account.

Reality: The concept of a "trust fund" implies, at least to most Americans, that the fund contains sufficient assets to meet its present and future obligations. The whole idea behind a trust is to put money into a fund for the purpose of letting the principal grow and earn interest so that it will accumulate assets to meet short-term and long-term commitments. It would only seem natural, then, to assume that a Social Security trust fund would contain tax revenues for Social Security benefits, and that those revenues would be invested in order to accumulate additional assets. But that's not the case.

As pointed out earlier, tax revenues are collected and used on a pay-as-you-go basis. A portion of the revenues are used to pay current Social Security benefits to qualified recipients, and the rest is put into the general revenue fund to be used as the federal government sees fit. There are no assets in a trust account accumulating interest or growing at a compound rate. In fact, the Secretary of the Treasury issues an IOU for the amount of the revenues that go into the general fund, and the transaction is recorded as a ledger book entry. At present, the U.S. government owes the Social Security trust fund account $1.7 trillion, and the debt grows by about $200 billion a year.[5] If the trust fund assets were actually needed, Treasury securities would have to be sold to secure the assets. And current estimates project that those assets could be needed as early as 2018.[6]

Perception: You have a legal right to your Social Security benefits.

Reality: Since most Americans view Social Security as an entitlement program, they feel they have a right to the benefits. But the fact is the federal government can reduce or remove benefits whenever it chooses — and it already has. Congress can abolish Social Security benefits if it chooses, but is unlikely to do so especially for lower-income retirees. Congress can also cut benefits as it did during the Reagan administration. To save Social Security assets, Congress changed the age at which one can collect full benefits from 65 to 67, effectively cutting benefits for workers born after 1939. And the U.S. Supreme Court has ruled that no one has a valid legal claim to Social Security benefits.[7]

Perception: Social Security is America's biggest budget deficit headache.

Reality: Social Security has gotten the lion's share of media attention and public scrutiny in recent years, but the bigger ticking time bomb in the federal budget is Medicare. Annual spending on Medicare alone is projected to be $500 billion more than that spent on Social Security by 2015. The projected shortfall in Social Security is somewhere between $10 and $12 trillion, depending on whose numbers you accept. However, this is dwarfed by the projected shortfall in Medicare, which is somewhere in the neighborhood of $62 trillion.[8] The cost of Medicare's promised benefits is expected to be $28 trillion more than its revenues over the next 75 years: five times more than Social Security's shortfall.[9]

Perception: Social Security is income tax free.

Reality: Social Security benefits were not originally taxed. But during the Reagan administration, the Greenspan Commission recommended that benefits be taxed, with the taxes used as a source of funding for Social Security. Initially, only half of the benefit could be taxed; now up to 85 percent may be taxed, depending on income and marital status.[10] Again, this amounts to a cut in benefits.

Growth In Social Security Expenditures	
Year	Expenditures in Millions
1938	$10
1958	$8,900
1968	$30,300
1978	$114,000
2004	$488,000
2005*	$518,000

*Estimate based on Michele Singletary, "After 70 Years, Social Security Still a Savior for Millions," *The Denver Post,* August 14, 2005

What started as a program to create jobs during the Great Depression has turned into a "perceived" retirement program that provides varying degrees of benefits to all Americans. This symbol of the New Deal has taken on the dimensions of an entitlement program that Americans seem to expect the government to provide forever. And it is precisely because of this belief that the program faces an uncertain, controversial future.

Is There a Crisis?
Americans are very protective of Social Security. It is the only remaining program of the New Deal era, and we are reluctant to even admit that there may be a problem with it. In fact, most Americans do not believe President Bush or members of Congress when they talk about a coming crisis for Social Security. After all, millions of us are counting on Social Security during our retirement years. Yet all is not well with the program. Indeed, a *Time* magazine survey showed that a majority of workers — 53 percent — had no confidence that Social Security could provide full benefits when they retired.[11]

How It Looks Today
Although workers are expected to pay anywhere from 25 to 40 percent of their incomes into Social Security and Medicare, just to keep them solvent, Social Security was never intended to be enough to provide a retirement for the American worker.[12] Yet, nearly two-thirds of retirees rely on Social Security for 50 percent of their retirement income, 33 percent rely on it for 90 percent or more of their retirement income, and 50 percent of retirees would live in poverty without Social Security.[13]

Social Security has grown into what is possibly the world's largest social welfare program. Total expenditures have grown from a meager $10 million in 1938[14] to over $500 billion in 2005. That's approximately 23 percent of the federal budget.[15] To support these expenditures, workers pay a substantial amount into the program. In fact, it has been estimated that as many as 80 percent of American workers pay more Social Security taxes than income taxes.[16] In return, American workers do receive a lot from Social Security. It has been estimated that an individual worker would have to save an additional $250,000 to replace the Social Security benefits he or she would receive if he or she lived the average retirement lifespan.[17]

Yet, that amount is simply insufficient to support most workers in their retirement. For example, the average monthly benefit at the end of 2004 was only $954, which comes out to less than $12,000 a year.[18] According to the House Ways and Means Committee, which has jurisdiction over Social Security, more than two million workers are collecting Social Security benefits that aren't enough to keep them above the poverty level, even though these workers have paid into the program throughout their working years. If proposed cuts are adopted, average-wage workers (those earning about $36,000) will see a 16 percent cut in benefits, while higher earning workers (those earning above $59,000) will see a 25 percent cut in benefits. It appears that the more you earn and pay into Social Security, the more your benefits are cut.[19] And the situation promises to worsen in the near future.

Social Security beneficiaries received a 4.1 percent cost of living increase on January 1, 2006, the biggest increase since a 5.4 percent boost in 1991. This will raise the average monthly benefit check to around $1,002 — the average retired couple, both receiving benefits, will see a jump from $1,583 to $1,648 per month. But before anyone gets overly excited about this newfound wealth, about 25 percent of it will be eaten up by an increase in Medicare premiums and higher energy costs are likely to eat up most of the rest.[20] But at least benefits went up rather than down.

Unplugged Leaks

Social Security's future is threatened by several factors of which the following three are most critical. First is the increasing longevity of elderly people. In 1935 when Social Security began, an average worker at age 65 could expect to live another 11.9 years in retirement. By the year 2040, officials project that an average worker at age 65 can expect to live another 19.7 years in retirement.[21] This added longevity puts an additional burden on Social Security by having to pay out more benefits to the average worker over a longer period of time.

Second is the bulge in the number of retired people. Not only are retired people living longer, there will be more of them over the next 20 years as 77 million Baby Boomers retire. The amount of benefits paid annually will increase sharply as the over-65 population becomes a significant percentage of the U.S. population. And as benefits increase across a larger number of elderly, so will almost every measure of disability, dependence and health-related expenses.[22]

Finally, the "dependency ratio," which is the number of workers supporting people collecting Social Security benefits, is declining at a critical rate. As life expectancies have increased, the ratio has declined to 3.25 workers supporting each beneficiary in 2005. Estimates place the dependency ratio at 2 workers to 1 beneficiary by the year 2030.[23] In any kind of shared benefit program, such as defined benefit pension plans or Social Security, the ability of the program to sustain benefits to retirees depends on the continued contributions of workers to the program. As the ratio of workers to retirees declines, it becomes increasingly difficult to support the benefits paid out to retirees — a very critical issue for Social Security.

Clearly, pressure is being applied to the Social Security program. Every year the program pays out more benefits to more retirees, survivors and disabled people. But there are fewer workers paying into the system compared to the benefits paid out. While the program is currently taking in more than it's paying out, most observers believe that ratio will change, probably around 2018 if recent estimates are correct. Traditional approaches to the problem, such as increased payroll taxes or cuts in Social Security benefits, may not be able to support the program at that time.

So What Does the Future Hold?
Overall, Social Security's unfunded liabilities total nearly $12 trillion. And estimates project that with each year we wait to reform the program the costs continue to climb by as much as $600 billion.[24] If we project out to the year 2075, and add Medicare to Social Security costs, it is estimated that the U.S. government will be spending as much as 20 percent of the national income on these two programs alone. Most observers believe this will be unsustainable.[25]

The cost of the full complement of federally funded entitlement programs — Social Security, Medicare and Medicaid — now totals 12.5 percent of GDP. Estimates project that by 2040 it will have almost doubled to 21.7 percent of GDP. In 2002, the shortfall in Social Security and Medicare was eight times the amount of total government spending. That's approximately $200,000 per U.S. household, or double the value of all stocks, bonds and mutual funds owned by American investors.[26] In 2004, these three government programs accounted for more than $1 trillion of the $2.2 trillion spent by the federal government.[27]

We cannot tax our way out of this deficit. According to the Social Security Administration, just financing the projected increases in Social Security and Medicare alone would require payroll tax increases of 50 percent by 2020, and by 200 to 300 percent by 2040.[28] And according to James Lockhart, Social Security

Deputy Commissioner, it will take $10.4 trillion in today's dollars for Social Security to attain sustainable solvency. That's equal to $100,000 per family.[29]

For Boomers, Social Security is not a good retirement investment. There is an expectation of potentially losing money, especially if Congress does raise payroll taxes or increases the cap on FICA wages to keep the program from going broke. In a 2005 report, the Social Security trustees stated that the money paid out in benefits would begin to exceed the payroll tax revenue by 2018. To continue to fully fund benefits, Social Security will have to tap into the trust fund, which has over $1 trillion dollars in Treasury securities. However, without some change or reform, the Social Security trust fund will be exhausted sometime around 2042. By that time the proportion of the population 65 and older will have doubled, and there won't be enough younger workers to fund the full range of benefits owed to retiring workers.[30] Benefits may not cease in 2042, but they can be seriously curtailed. Because Social Security will continue to collect payroll taxes, it will be able to pay an estimated 70 percent of currently legislated benefits.[31]

In Need of Reform

What we currently have is a system where the average benefit recipient gets more than he or she has paid in, a system with no real assets, and a system that depends on workers paying taxes to support retired workers. Whatever balance this system had, it is quickly disappearing as retirees grow in number and live longer in retirement.[32] According to former Federal Reserve Chair, Alan Greenspan, raising national savings is a must. We must build capital stock by 2030 that will be large enough to provide retirees with the products and services they need without curbing the standard of living for the working population. The current Social Security system has not proven a reliable vehicle for such saving.[33]

At present, Social Security is operating on faulty principles. It lacks fairness and it seems to have few logical underpinnings that would provide a strong foundation for a secure future. Social Security can't possibly keep from going broke when it pays out far more than it takes in. Retirees counting on Social Security for the majority of their retirement income are very likely to face some frightening years ahead.

Most observers agree that Social Security is in need of reform. A survey of members of the Financial Planning Association (FPA) showed that 92.6 percent agreed that something must be done to fix Social Security to prevent it from going broke.[34] But when it comes to discussing system reforms, the fastest way to end a conversation is to mention the words "Social Security." Even Republicans, who generally detest a welfare state, find it difficult to launch proposals to change Social Security.

Any plan to change Social Security, if it is to appear credible, will likely require some combination of retirement-age shifts, benefit-level changes or further government borrowing.[35] However, key legislators believe that Congress does not have the political will to cut benefits and increase taxes sufficiently to make Social Security self-sustaining. It is much more likely to develop a package of cuts in current benefits that would increase the system's viability for several more decades.[36] But that future increase does nothing to help strengthen the retirement incomes of those who largely depend on Social Security.

At the beginning of his second term, President Bush pushed for legislation that would permit workers to put up to four percent of their FICA payroll taxes in private accounts. While this may look good on the surface, there are two major drawbacks. First, private accounts will not solve the Social Security problem. In fact, they will exacerbate it. Private accounts divert taxes from current retiree benefits, bringing the end of Social Security surpluses closer to reality.

Second, private accounts, which are simply defined contribution plans like 401(k)s and put the burden on investors rather than the government, something that companies have also done by freezing defined pension programs. Studies show that when given the chance to make choices, most Americans don't stray from a basic index fund. They tend to continue chasing last year's returns, stick with stocks too long after they have peaked, or invest too conservatively without diversifying.[37]

Despite several months of promoting across the U.S., support for the President's private retirement accounts was not forthcoming. In the fall of 2005, President Bush finally admitted that he had given up on the private accounts idea, and that his willingness to continue to push for Social Security reform had seriously diminished.[38]

As the country readies itself for the political battles of the 2006 midterm election campaigns, most observers believe that any attempt to reform Social Security will wait for a few more years. Senator Charles Grassley (R-Iowa), Senate Finance Committee chairman, recently stated that Social Security reform is likely tabled until after President Bush's second term ends in 2009. He believes that the 2006 midterm elections and the next presidential election in 2008 are likely to prevent any action since reform is such a sensitive political issue. In effect, this means that Social Security's current situation has four more years to deteriorate before any additional attempt is made to address it.[39]

Whenever reform finally does come, it is unlikely that the problems of Social Security can be solved by traditional methods. But there is one likely prediction we should take seriously. The Congressional Budget Office estimates with a high degree of confidence that Social Security and Medicare will consume an increasing share of the federal budget.[40] So without some type of reform, retirees will be able to count on Social Security less, and the federal debt will continue to rise. Given such circumstances, Social Security cannot be the foundation for any serious retirement plan.

[1] "Greenspan on Budget Policy," *The Wall Street Journal Online*, December 2, 2005.

[2] Martin Crutsinger, "Millions to Receive Social Security Boost," *Associated Press*, October 15, 2005.

[3] Brooke Oberwetter, "Social Security: The Shoebox Approach," *www.cato.org*, February 14, 2005.

[4] Peter J. Ferrara, "Social Security: The Inherent Contradiction," Cato Institute, 1980.

[5] Oberwetter, op. cit.

[6] James B. Lockhart III, "Strengthening Social Security," Social Security Administration, March 21, 2005.

[7] Mike Clowes, "Real Risk for Social Security Is Legislation," *Investment News*, September 5, 2005.

[8] "[Social Security] A National Obsession . . . But What About the 'Gorilla in the Closet'?" Jackson National Life Insurance Company, 2004.

[9] "Scary Numbers," *St. Petersburg Times*, June 26, 2005.

[10] Clowes, op. cit.

[11] Karen Tumulty and Eric Roston, "Is There Really a Crisis?" *Time*, January 16, 2005.

[12] Robert Brokamp, "Why You Hate, and Like, Social Security," *The Motley Fool*, September 16, 2004.

[13] Social Security Administration, 2004.

[14] Ferrara, op. cit.

[15] "Budgetary Perspectives on the Outlook for Social Security," Congressional Budget Office Testimony, February 9, 2005.

[16] Robert Brokamp, "Retirement's First Leg: Social Security," *The Motley Fool*, July 1, 2004.

[17] "Social Security: More Than You Might Think," AARP, 2004.

[18] Robert Brokamp, "7 Social Security Myths," *The Motley Fool*, February 3, 2005.

[19] "Hitting the Middle Class, Again," *The New York Times*, May 3, 2005.

[20] Crutsinger, op. cit.

[21] Peter G. Peterson, *Running on Empty*, Picador, 2004.

[22] Ibid.

[23] "Greenspan," op. cit.

[24] "Signs of Crisis Are Clear," Cato Institute, February 1, 2005.

[25] "Graying of America," NewsHour With Jim Lehrer Transcript, May 25, 2005.

[26] Peterson, op. cit.

[27] "U.S. Census Bureau Tip Sheet: Consolidated Federal Funds Report for Fiscal Year 2004," *U.S. Newswire*, December 27, 2005.

[28] Ibid.

[29] Lockhart, op. cit.

[30] Brokamp, op. cit.

[31] Greg Crawford and Vineeta Anand, "Retirement Disaster: Defining the 3 Legs of the Stool ... or Should it Be 4?" *Pensions & Investments*, April 18, 2005.

[32] Bill Mann, "On Social Security: Fun With Numbers," *The Motley Fool*, February 28, 2005.

[33] "Greenspan," op. cit.

[34] "FPA Members Strongly Favor Social Security Reforms," *FANews*, June 22, 2005.

[35] Jackie Calmes, "Ambitions to Fix Social Security Present Big Hurdles for Bush," *The Wall Street Journal Online*, September 2, 2004.

[36] "What a Social Security Deal Could Look Like," *BusinessWeek Online*, May 30, 2005.

[37] Karen Tumulty and Eric Roston, op. cit.

[38] "Social Security Reform Dead Until '09?" *Ignites*, November 9, 2005.

[39] Ibid.

[40] "The Not-So-Incredible Shrinking Deficit," *The Economist.com*, August 16, 2005.

Taxes represent the average American household's single largest expense.

Chapter Four ◀

The Tax Axe

Do you know how much of your income goes to taxes? Taxation is a factor that will affect everyone's retirement, no matter how wealthy they are. Taxation poses a major threat to your financial security, not only during your retirement but also right now as you plan and save. Taxes have taken an increasing portion of Americans' income over the years. Combined federal, state and local taxes per capita have increased from 24.6 percent of average income in 1950, to nearly 30 percent in 2005, and actually exceeded 33 percent in 2000.

America's Growing Tax Burden	
Year	**Taxes as a Percentage of Income**
1900	5.9%
1910	5.0%
1920	11.6%
1930	11.2%
1940	17.6%
1950	24.6%
1960	27.4%
1970	29.4%
1980	30.3%
1990	30.5%
2000	33.6%
2001	32.6%
2002	29.8%
2003	28.9%
2004	28.6%
2005	29.1%

Sources: Office of Management and Budget; Internal Revenue Service; Congressional Research Service; National Bureau of Economic Research; Tax Foundation, 2005

Taxes represent the average American household's single largest monthly expense, almost twice as much as the next highest expense: housing.[1] Today, the typical American family now spends more on income tax than it does on food, clothing and transportation combined.

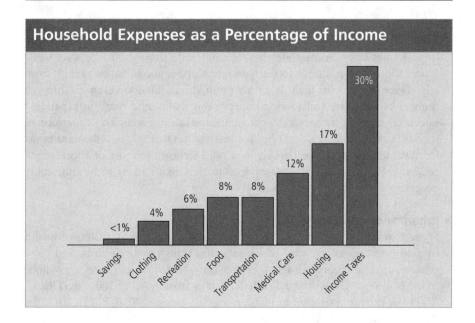

Household Expenses as a Percentage of Income

Savings: <1%
Clothing: 4%
Recreation: 6%
Food: 8%
Transportation: 8%
Medical Care: 12%
Housing: 17%
Income Taxes: 30%

Income taxes are only the beginning. Americans are also paying an additional array of taxes, including:

- **State Income Tax**
  In 2005, 41 states collected personal income tax; 35 of those based the taxes on your federal returns, either by collecting a direct portion of your federal payment or by using your federal adjusted gross income or taxable income as a starting point.

- **Property Tax**
  Property taxes are levied not by states but by local governments and form their biggest source of revenue. These taxes are usually assessed on a portion of market value and exist in some form everywhere in the United States. Property taxes have been rising dramatically. Between 2000 and 2004, median family income rose just 8 percent. But among the largest expense increases (including healthcare premiums, college tuition and gasoline) were property taxes, which rose by 30 percent.[2] Certainly, in most states it may be possible to gain a property tax break based on your age; however, the system may still seem quite unfair, not only to retirees but to most homeowners. Indeed, financial publishers at Kiplinger have noted, "Soaring tax bills are fueling revolts by homeowners squeezed by taxes on paper profits that they may never be able to realize."[3]

- **Sales Tax**

   All states except Alaska, Delaware, Montana, New Hampshire and Oregon impose sales taxes. Some states have a single rate throughout the state while others allow local additions to the base rate. Certain goods can be exempt from sales taxes: these may include prescription drugs, food or even clothing. A number of states are considering tax revisions that would result in expanding sales taxes to more services, rather than just the sale of goods. This expansion of service taxes may be a critical need for many states that rely heavily on sales tax for revenue, but will likely result in a tax increase for most of those states' residents. Services from dry cleaning to gardening are likely to become more expensive under these proposals.

- **Inheritance and Estate Tax**

   Some states still collect an inheritance tax, but in every state, transfers of wealth to a spouse are tax exempt. In some states, transfers to children and close relatives are also exempt. Currently, estate tax rates fall under the tax provisions of the Economic Growth and Tax Relief Reconciliation Act of 2001 (EGTRRA). EGTRRA is temporarily set to phase out estate taxes in 2010. But in 2011, the 2003 effective rates will be restored.[4]

Who Is Paying America's Taxes?

It is often said that the wealthiest people in the United States do not pay much income tax: they seem to take advantage of all the loopholes with the assistance of creative accountants. We also often hear that it is the middle-income and upper-middle-income Americans who pay the most. Paying America's taxes is a huge burden; one that is not evenly distributed. For example, some 40 percent of Americans pay no income tax at all, which in 2004 amounted to around 44 million people.[5] The fact is, whether or not you believe the nation's super wealthy can afford to pay more taxes, the higher the income, the greater the tax burden.

The Increasing Tax Burden on "the Rich"

The bulk of the nation's tax burden is shouldered by a small percentage of Americans. According to the Tax Foundation, a non-partisan tax research organization based in Washington D.C., if you shrunk the taxpaying public to a microcosm of 100 taxpayers, you would find that one of them is paying a full 36 percent of the federal tax bill, up from 25 percent in 1986. Forty-nine of them are paying 60 percent of the bill. The bottom half or the remaining 50 of these 100 people pay only four percent of the federal tax bill.

The tax burden for so-called "upper income" taxpayers has escalated over the years. The top 10 percent of income earners in 1981 were responsible for about 48 percent of all federal income taxes. In 1991, that responsibility had grown to 56 percent. By 2001, the top 10 percent of income earners paid 65 percent of the nation's tax burden.[6] Who knows what the percentage will be in the future? I don't know, but this situation contains both good and bad news. The good news is that the government has been and is continuing to increase the tax burden on the rich. That sounds only fair, right?

But the bad news is, *you're* rich. You may not consider yourself rich, but if you earned more than $57,343 in 2003, you were in the top 25 percent of all American taxpayers, and you can be sure that your tax burden is growing right along with that of the top 1 percent.[7]

Income Levels of America's Top Taxpayers (2003)	
If Your Annual Income Is...	**Where Does That Place You Among America's Taxpayers?**
$295,495	Top 1%
$130,080	Top 5%
$94,891	Top 10%
$57,343	Top 25%
$29,019	Top 50%

So if people like you and me are now classified as rich, shouldn't there be a separate tax for the super rich? There is. It's called the Alternative Minimum Tax (AMT). This is a federal tax that was created around 1969 to prevent high-income earners from avoiding significant tax liability by abusing exclusions, deductions and tax credits to minimize their taxes. High-income earners may get thrown into AMT when they take numerous deductions or when they receive a significant income increase—such as exercising a large block of stock options. AMT results in the taxpayer losing many of the historic tax breaks: property taxes, state and city income taxes, exemptions for children, and interest on home-equity loans.

Once you are subject to AMT, not only will you have to pay more federal tax, but you'll also pay 100 cents on the dollar for every increase in rapidly rising property and state taxes. AMT is a sneak attack, with stricter rules for deductions and credits than those most of us obey. But here's some more bad news: The number of Americans impacted by AMT has been growing steadily and is set to triple in the next five years.[8] How soon will it be before you join their number?

Taxes and Retirement Income

Let's take a look at what taxes can do to your retirement income. There is a common misconception that once you retire you start paying less in taxes, if any at all, simply because you're no longer working a full-time job and you're in a lower tax bracket. Don't assume, however, that your taxes will be lower in retirement. It's not easy to live on the reduced income needed to qualify for this apparent tax advantage. Furthermore, you'll need to earn more income every year just to keep pace with inflation. So even if you begin your retirement in a lower tax bracket, watch out; you may migrate into a higher one.

Here's a chilling statistic: In 2003, some 24 percent of owners of taxable fixed income fund shares lost 45 percent of their returns to taxes. Even in a year with the second lowest amount of capital gains and dividends since 1995, all fund investors paid a total of around $6.5 billion in taxes. Mutual fund intelligence firm Lipper called this a "conservative estimate."[9] These sobering numbers make it difficult to accept the notion of lower taxes in retirement.

Can Social Security Benefits Really Be Taxed?

Yes. It's quite ironic that, having paid taxes throughout your working life to fund Social Security, you may then find yourself having to pay federal income tax on your Social Security benefits. It's hard to believe, but as much as 85 percent of your benefits could be subject to income taxes depending on the amount of income you earn during retirement.[10] The formula used is complicated: Your retirement income is calculated by adding any annual income from pensions, wages, dividends or interest, to 50 percent of your Social Security benefits. The formula then factors in any tax-exempt interest income, such as that from municipal bonds. The total is called your "modified adjusted gross income." If that amount is more than $34,000 for single persons or $44,000 for married couples filing jointly, your Social Security benefits could be taxed up to 85 percent.

Planning and Taxes

Unfortunately, planning for retirement is not a simple matter of figuring how to avoid paying taxes. Rather, it is a question of tax management. Let me give a word of caution. Qualified retirement plans—employer-sponsored retirement plans like profit-sharing or 401(k)s, or individually owned accounts like IRAs, or tax-exempt investments like municipal bond funds—offer certain tax advantages that make them attractive investments for retirement planning. However, you need to realize that taxes and penalties might apply to withdrawals from IRAs or from other retirement accounts such as annuities. For example, tax-deferred plans carry a 10 percent federal tax penalty for what are considered "early withdrawals." These are withdrawals made by the account owner before age 59½. There are exceptions for some events, including death and disability, and this penalty can be avoided if the account owner takes what are called "substantially equal periodic payments" over his or her life expectancy.

You should also note that an investment free of federal income tax, such as a municipal bond, can still be subject to state and local taxes, as well as the dreaded AMT, and is not appropriate for a tax-deferred account. And if you want to purchase taxable investments for retirement, you may be subject to income tax from the dividends generated, as well as capital gains taxes. That is why it's important to build your retirement plan around a sound consideration of what you expect for your after-tax returns. Remember, if you dip into your investments to pay the taxes on them, the amount of money you actually get to spend now, as well as later, will be reduced.

The Importance of Tax Deferral

As you endure the slow and often painful process of accumulating assets for retirement, it is useful to keep an eye on what your savings are doing, and to consider what they may not be doing. I am referring to tax deferral, which should be, and yet is surprisingly lacking, an essential component in anyone's retirement plan. Quite simply, tax deferral is what happens when an investment, such as a retirement account, is allowed to grow without being taxed. Earnings are withdrawn after compounded interest is allowed to do its job. Given the same annual rate of return, tax-deferred assets will increase more rapidly than currently taxable assets, assuming these are used to pay the taxes.

Tax deferral is a feature common to many tax-qualified retirement plans such as IRAs, 401(k)s and Keogh plans. However, many of these plans have annual contribution limits and, even if you are eligible, they will not provide a complete solution for your retirement savings. Other savings vehicles, such as annuities, also grow tax-deferred. Of course, when selecting an appropriate investment for your retirement, it is important to discuss your situation and needs with a professional financial adviser.

For now, let's assume that you and your adviser are creating a suitable plan for reaching your retirement goals. One important consideration is that a large portion of your withdrawals from retirement savings are likely to be taxable. But can you predict how high those taxes will be?

Tax Rate Risk

Most of us know of the major risks investors face. There's market risk and interest rate risk, but we may be overlooking another quite significant risk: Tax rate risk. Tax rates are something over which we have no control. And no matter what kind of vehicle you invest in for retirement, future tax rates will have an enormous impact on how much of your savings you will actually be able to spend when the time comes.

When we save with a tax-deferred account, tax rate risk becomes one of the biggest risks we face. Quite simply, it's the danger that an increase in income tax rates during your retirement could cost you a lot of money and hurt your retirement lifestyle by lowering the net amount of your withdrawals. Studies show that income tax rates fluctuate over time, and even when the stated rates don't seem to change, the effective tax rate on your personal taxable income may increase when the government increases, restricts or repeals tax benefits. Such changes could occur in the size of the personal exemption, itemized deductions, tax credits, exclusions from income, and other areas. Today's stated income tax rates may be historically low compared to the last 50 years, but there is always a chance that they will rise.

Why should you worry about taxes now? Because you may be depositing money into a qualified plan in order to avoid current taxation. But by the time you retire and begin taking money out, your effective income tax rate might have increased. Once this increase happens, there's nothing you can do about it. You have to pay tax at the rates in effect when you make your withdrawals. What happens then? Do you delay your withdrawals for as long as possible? Or should you at least keep them as small as possible in the hope that income tax rates will decrease sometime soon? Of course, this tactic may not enable you to live the kind of retirement lifestyle you originally dreamt of. Since the advantages of tax-deferral are fairly clear for most people, there may be little you can do about tax rate risk, except remain aware of all your options.

Converting a traditional IRA into an account that generates tax-free returns, such as a Roth IRA, is a taxable event. The Roth IRA can address potential income tax rate risk, but then it can't solve the issue of estate tax rate risk. An increase in estate taxes would affect the size of your account balance available to pass on to your loved ones.

Just like income tax rates, history shows us that estate tax rates rise and fall over time. Currently, estate tax rates fall under the tax provisions of EGTRRA. But as we have noted, EGTRRA's provisions are only temporary: they are set to phase out in 2010, but in 2011, the 2003 effective rates will be restored, which are significantly higher than the 2009 rates. To put it simply, compared to today's rates, estate tax rates will increase.

What Else Can They Tax Us On – The Air We Breathe?

Sometimes it seems that way. Last week I received my phone bill. I usually just check it to make sure that I recognize all the calls I'm being charged for and that the services I'm paying for are the services I actually subscribe to. But this time, I paused over the section I suspect most of us ignore, the one called "Government Fees and Taxes." I should not have been surprised to see that I was paying surcharges and taxes, but I was amazed by how many of these charges there were. All in all, there were nine such items. In addition to the various fees such as "Universal Lifeline Surcharge," I saw that I was paying federal tax, local tax and utility users tax. That's just for having a telephone.

Despite all the attention given to federal income taxes, they represent only 42 percent of the total tax burden Americans carry each year.[11] Americans face a variety of "hidden" taxes, from sales tax to property tax to utility taxes.

Let's take a look at some common hidden taxes. They will of course vary from state to state, and if location is an important part of your retirement dream, you should consider the tax implications very carefully.

- **Social Security Tax**
  Each paycheck you receive has a portion taken out for Social Security, otherwise known as FICA. Social Security is funded through employment taxes of 12.4 percent of wages. Your employer pays half, or 6.2 percent, and you pay the other half.

- **Medicare Tax**
  The Medicare tax rate is currently 2.9 percent for both you and your employer (1.45 percent each).

- **Marriage License Tax**
  When a couple decides to get married they are assessed a fee for getting married. That's right; you can't get married without a license, and you have to pay a fee for that privilege.

- **Liquor Tax**
  Every bottle of alcohol you buy is levied with a liquor tax.

- **Toll Road Booth Tax**
  You may live in a state, such as New Jersey and Massachusetts, where every time you want to get on the highway, you pay a toll to access that road. Good luck if you don't have change.

- **Toll Bridge Tax**
  Try to get on or off the island of Manhattan without paying a toll bridge fee. If you don't have your own boat to take you from one part of an island to another, you could pay a toll bridge tax.

- **Gasoline Tax**
  All states collect fuel taxes and some may even allow cities or counties to collect local fuel taxes as well. There are also federal excise taxes on gasoline, diesel and ethanol. If you want to avoid paying a fuel tax, you probably won't be driving your car.

"Hidden" Taxes

Accounts Receivable Tax	Social Security Tax
Amusement Tax	Sparkler and Novelties Tax
Blueberry Tax	Tattoo Tax
Building Permit Tax	Telephone Federal Excise Tax
Corporate Income Tax	Telephone Federal Tax
Flush Tax	Telephone Federal Universal Service Tax
Fountain Soda Tax	Telephone State and Local Tax
Fuel Permit Tax	Toll Bridge Tax
Fur Clothing Tax	Toll Road Booth Tax
Gasoline Tax	Trailer Registration Tax
Inheritance Tax	Utilities Tax
Liquor Tax	Vehicle License Registration Tax
Marriage License Tax	Vehicle Sales Tax
Medicare Tax	Wagering Tax
Recreational Vehicle Tax	Watercraft Registration Tax
Road Usage Tax	Well Permit Tax
Septic Permit Tax	
Service Charge Tax	

• Retirement Income Tax

Fifteen states currently tax Social Security benefits — in addition to federal income tax — though most of these states will exempt at least a portion of pension income from taxable income, depending on the type of pension. If states exempt the pensions of state and local government retirees, they are generally prohibited from taxing the benefits of U.S. military retirees.

The average American's total tax burden is a whopping 56 percent of their personal spending,[12] which means we spend half a year working to pay taxes. This tax burden may indeed be one reason why Americans seem to have so much difficulty saving money and why our country has one of the lowest personal savings rates in the developed world.

Mr. and Mrs. Jones

Here's a brainteaser: When is a tax deduction not a savings? Before you start to answer that, you also need to bear in mind that during your retirement years you may not see as many tax deductions as you enjoyed while you were working. Certainly, there is the standard deduction for people aged 65 and older. But one of the most significant deductions for so many American families has been the federal income tax deduction on mortgage interest paid. For this very reason, along with historically low mortgage rates, many seniors are carrying their mortgage debt well into their retirement years.

Yet there are times when this mortgage interest tax strategy can turn out to have quite a different effect for retirees. For example, take the case of Mr. and Mrs. Jones, a retired couple who own their home outright and live comfortably off just enough Social Security benefits and IRA withdrawals to meet annual living expenses of $39,000. But what if Mr. and Mrs. Jones still had a mortgage? Even with a low fixed-rate loan, they would still need enough after-tax income to cover their living expenses and their mortgage payments. Not only that, they will find that their mortgage interest deduction may decrease over time as their amortized payments increasingly consist of principal instead of interest. Thus, at some point, the standard deduction may be more beneficial to them than claiming the mortgage interest on Schedule A.

Indeed, to continue meeting their expenses, the Jones may have to increase the size of their IRA withdrawals. The withdrawals will accelerate the depletion of their nest egg, increase their annual income tax, and could bump them to a higher income tax bracket, thus increasing their federal income tax bill. The withdrawals also divert money away from addressing healthcare costs, a major expense for retirees, to paying Uncle Sam. What started out as a smart decision to take advantage of a tax deduction, soon turned into a financial disaster. And, yes, Mr. and Mrs. Jones may end up paying income tax on 50 percent of their Social Security benefits because their income may exceed the provisional income level that protected them from income taxation.

[1] Tax Foundation, Special Report No. 112, April 2003.

[2] "The Real Middle Class Squeeze," *Business Week*, August 2, 2004.

[3] "Taxes," *The Kiplinger Letter*, Vol. 82, No. 23, June 10, 2005.

[4] Individual State Tax and Revenue Departments; State Tax Handbook (2005); published by CCH Inc.; Federation of Tax Administrators; The Tax Foundation; National Conference of State Legislatures; The Tax Foundation; National Conference of State Legislatures; U.S. Department of Commerce, Bureau of Economic Analysis.

[5] "Summary of Federal Individual Income Tax Data," Tax Foundation, *www.taxfoundation.org*, October 11, 2005.

[6] U.S. Treasury, Office of Tax Analysis (April 2004).

[7] Tax Foundation (October 2005).

[8] Tax Policy Center, Joint Venture of the Urban Institute and Brookings Institution, 2005.

[9] Financial Planning, Lipper, April 19, 2004.

[10] IRS, Publication 915, 2003.

[11] Institute for Policy Innovation, "Hidden Taxes: How Much Do You Really Pay?" August 29, 2001.

[12] Bryan Riley, Eric V. Schlecht, Dr. John Berhoud, "Hidden Taxes: How Much Do You Really Pay?" Institute For Policy Innovations Policy Report 160 (July 2001).

*Today it takes $2.20 to buy
what $1 bought in 1980.*

Chapter Five ◀
Inflation — The Invisible Enemy

So far we have talked about a few of the major risks involved in planning for a retirement. There's longevity: the likelihood that you'll live to a ripe old age and not have enough money to fund your long retirement. Then there are taxes: insidious to many, and unavoidable to us all. But there's another factor that many people ignore. This factor, driven purely by economic forces, has no visible impact on the actual dollar amounts you save before retirement or receive during retirement. This "invisible enemy," the fifth challenge to your retirement, is inflation. The problem with inflation is that it sneaks up on you. Inflation can't be sent as a payment deducted from your paycheck or sent as a payment to the government. But if you forget about inflation altogether, its effect on your retirement lifestyle can be catastrophic. And yet very few people ever stop to consider the severity of inflation's impact.

As most of us know, inflation is quite simply what happens when prices go up. For example, in 1934, a first-class postage stamp cost three cents. Today, it costs 39 cents. That's a total inflation for the stamp of some 1,300 percent,[1] an annual increase of 18.6%. Now of course, that increase is still just a few cents. Most of us would hope to afford a postage stamp, no matter how much it goes up over time. But what about all the other goods and services that are going up in price along with the stamp? Take just the last 40 years as an example:

The Sting of Inflation

Item	Cost in 1965	Cost in 2002	Overall Price Increase	Average Annual Price Increase
New Ford Mustang	$2,427	$17,475	650%	5.48%
A New House	$20,000	$161,000	705%	5.79%
A Day in Hospital	$41	$3,533	8,517%	12.8%

Source: Kelley Blue Book, Ibbotson Associates, 2004; U.S. Department of Labor, Bureau of Labor Statistics; Mutual of Omaha, 2004

Measuring Inflation

Inflation is measured by taking a basket of goods, and comparing its average prices at two intervals in time, while adjusting for changes made to those goods. When planning for retirement, the measure of inflation you need to be most concerned with is consumer inflation as represented by changes in the Consumer Price Index (CPI). The CPI measures the price of a selection of goods purchased by a "typical consumer" — that's you — and is the most commonly reported inflation data in the United States. The annual *inflation rate* is the percentage rate of increase in this index.

We should note that there is no single true measure of inflation, because measures of inflation do depend on other things such as the relative weight given to each good in an index, as well as the characteristics of the economic region being measured. Other inflation measures used by economists include:

- **The Cost of Living Index (CLI).** This is the theoretical increase in the cost of living for an individual.

- **The Producer Price Index (PPI).** This measures changes in the prices received by producers and is different from the CPI, because subsidies, profits and taxes may cause the amounts received by producers to differ from the amounts consumers pay.

- **The Wholesale Price Index** looks at the change in wholesale prices for a selection of goods.

- **The Commodity Price Index** simply charts the changes in price of a selection of commodities.

When viewed over a length of time, measurements such as the CPI can produce some quite startling statistics.

What Does History Tell Us?
Since 1916, inflation, as measured by the CPI:

- Averaged 3.5 percent per year.
- Has been present in all but 11 years.
- Averaged 4.7 percent per year, when it occurred.

And to put inflation into perspective ...

- What $1 could buy in 1980 would cost more than $2.20 today.

So how worried should you be? Currently, you don't seem to be worried at all. Only about 9 percent of Americans seem to be concerned about how severely inflation could impact their retirement savings. A recent survey by the National Association for Variable Annuities (NAVA) showed that respondents from all age groups placed inflation at or near the bottom of their list of retirement worries. Perhaps this shouldn't be surprising since we have had quite low inflation rates in recent years.[2] But looking at just recent years' inflation is a dangerously short-term view.

Inflation can be somewhat predictable in the very short term, and I'm sure most of us are familiar with the Federal Reserve's periodic comments on it. But inflation's long-term behavior is less predictable and far more worrying. Look at the average annual rates of inflation for the last nine complete decades:

Decade	Average Annual Inflation Rate
1910s	14.57%
1920s	0%
1930s	-1.42%
1940s	-1.24%
1950s	0.69%
1960s	5.46%
1970s	11.35%
1980s	4.82%
1990s	2.21%

Source: Inflationdata.com

Inflation has not recently passed the 14.57 percent it averaged in the 1910s, but it did come close in the seventies. The thirties and forties both show negative annual inflation, but at what cost? The thirties was the decade of the Great Depression with its plummeting wages and prices, while the forties saw both World War II and a painfully slow recovery from the Depression. The more prosperous decades of the twentieth century, such as in the twenties, the fifties, and the nineties, have notably showed low inflation. The reality is that inflation has been a significant factor in our economic lives since at least the end of World War II. In fact, since 1950, the purchasing power of the dollar has diminished every year.

How Inflation Impacts Your Spending Power

Many financial advisers have told me that one of the most common errors people make in their retirement planning is to assume they should receive a fixed level of income for the duration of their retirement. Yet our "invisible enemy" proves just how dangerous this strategy can be. Why? Because inflation is practically guaranteed to erode your spending power. For example, if the annual inflation rate is 3 percent, a $1 candy bar will cost you $1.03 in a year's time. In other words, your dollar will no longer be able to pay for the candy bar. In practice you might be offered a smaller version of the same candy bar for your dollar, but that doesn't bode well for your retirement lifestyle when it comes to more important durable goods such as cars, or essential services such as healthcare.

When you see climbing store prices you are certainly aware that inflation is taking place. But you might also reasonably suppose that, if wages and prices increase at the same rate, it all balances out in the end. That sounds good, but the problem is, wages and prices are not both magically coupled to inflation. Wages are assumed by many to increase in line with inflation. It certainly makes sense that workers would not want to work for a decreasing income compared to what they need to spend. However, recent data tends to show that the wages and salaries of American workers are not keeping up with inflation. As recently as October 2005, the CPI was at 4 percent, whereas average wages in America rose by just 3.1 percent in the same month. During our working lives, we tend to adjust more easily to inflation; we modify our consumption, or we seek ways to increase our income. Some consumers even leverage inflation by assuming greater debt. But during retirement, increasing your debt is probably unwise because your income is something you may not have much control over.

Let's look at a serious example of what inflation can do to your retirement savings: Suppose you have $10,000 in the bank. At just a 3 percent inflation rate, which is the historical average since the twenties, the spending power of your $10,000 is reduced by 25 percent after 10 years, and cut almost in half after 20 years. And I offer a note of caution about the 3 percent historical average inflation rate. It dates back to 1916; however, we have seen that inflation has been dramatically higher as recently as the seventies.

Put another way, if you need $50,000 a year to live on today, assuming a 3 percent annual inflation rate, you'll need more than double that amount, $101,640, in 25 years, just to maintain the same lifestyle.[3]

How Much Could Your $10,000 Really Be Worth?

Annual Inflation Rate	Value of Nest Egg at Retirement	Value After 10 Years	After 20 Years	After 30 Years
3% (1990s)	$10,000	$7,441	$5,537	$4,120
5% (1980s)	$10,000	$6,139	$3,769	$2,314
11% (1970s)	$10,000	$3,522	$1,240	$437

If you're on a fixed income, as you may have planned for during retirement, you will suffer on account of inflation because the cost of goods you need to buy will increase while your income stays the same.

Can Anyone Stop Inflation?

How Inflation Reduces Your Real Income	
	Your Real Annual Retirement Income
Today	$50,000
10 Years From Now	$37,205
15 Years From Now	$32,093
20 Years From Now	$27,684

Assumes a three percent annual inflation rate

Economists suggest a number of methods to curb inflation. It is generally assumed that wages and prices will rise faster if aggregate demand is stimulated to stretch the labor and capital markets. Central banks such as our Federal Reserve try to influence inflation through what is known as monetary policy.

Monetary policy is the process whereby the country's money supply is manipulated to achieve specific goals, such as restricting inflation or stimulating employment or economic growth. A number of different tools, including changing interest rates or setting reserve requirements are used in monetary policy. The best known example is that of a central bank that raises interest rates, thus tightening the money supply to create a decline in production and check further price increases. In practice, this policy is realized through what we call "open market operations."

In the United States, the most common monetarist method used to address inflation is for the Federal Reserve to set a target for the federal funds rate — the interest rate at which member banks lend to one another overnight. You may recall from Fed statements made in 2005, concerns over inflation usually play a role in its decisions to raise the target rate, with the goal of achieving a lower rate of change in the CPI.

Between June 2003 and January 2006, the Federal Open Market Committee (FOMC) met 14 times to discuss the federal funds interest rate. Each of these 14 times, the committee voted to increase the federal funds rate by a quarter of a percent – from one percent to four and-a-half percent. Most investors were of the opinion that the rate had reached a point of balance in January 2006, and that future rate increases were not necessary, although they anticipated the committee might raise the rate one more time. Sure enough, citing worries over inflation, the committee met again in March 2006 and voted to increase the rate to four and three-quarters percent.

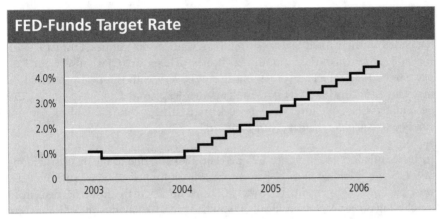

FED-Funds Target Rate

Note: Chart begins at March 28, 2003.
Source: Federal Reserve

Most disturbing to investors was the fact that the committee indicated that additional increases might be necessary to hold inflation in check. Investors are concerned that another increase would slow economic growth and weaken the market.

Why should you care about the relationship between inflation and interest rates? Because it shows you how much your money is really worth.

Real Interest Rates vs. Unreal Investment Assumptions

For the most part, demand for goods and services is not related to the nominal rates, which are the market interest rates quoted in the newspapers. Instead, it is related to what we call *real* interest rates. The real interest rate equals the nominal or stated interest rate *minus* the inflation rate.

For example, let's say you took out a car loan at 6 percent. You would probably feel happier about your loan rate if inflation were close to 11 percent (its average during the 1970s) than if inflation were near 2 percent (as in the 1990s). This is because in the first case, the real interest rate on your loan is – five percent (or six percent minus 11 percent), which means that the real value of the money you're paying back to your lender is lower than its real value when you borrowed it. In fact, it is highly unlikely that you would get such a good deal in that inflationary environment.

In the second, more likely, scenario, you are paying back a real interest rate of four percent (six percent minus two percent). The real value of the money you pay back is genuinely more than the real value of the money you borrowed. When it comes to what inflation can do to the real value of your investment returns, just remember that the real return on your investment is not how many more dollars are in your account, but how much you can actually buy with the money you have.

A High Return Is Not Always a High Return

To examine just how damaging inflation can be, take the example of what happened in the United States during the seventies and eighties. From 1970-74, the rate of return on six-month certificates of deposit (CDs) rose from 7.64 percent to 10.02 percent, something that was very enthusiastically received by many investors. In 1979, CD rates took another leap, from 11.42 percent, to 15.79 percent by 1981. Yet investors who celebrated these "returns" had clearly not stopped to calculate their *real rate of return.*[4]

In 1972, inflation was just over 3.25 percent. By 1974, due to the oil crisis among other things, it had risen to 11 percent. In 1980, it topped 13.5 percent, and, CDs were paying 12.94 percent. That year, CD investors actually lost 0.56 percent in purchasing power. More specifically, if you had put $10,000 into one of these CDs, your account statement would have shown $11,294 by the end of the year. While this may have looked encouraging, your money could only have purchased $9,769 worth of goods relative to the previous year's dollars. And don't forget, that return was before taxes!

Planning and Inflation

I hope by now that you understand how profoundly inflation will affect your ability to save and invest money. A critical issue in retirement planning is the way inflation erodes the purchasing power of retirement income. Inflation makes it imperative that you have diversified investments and sources of income; some sectors of the economy will outperform others at certain times, while the cost of living will continue its march upward.

Inflation doesn't stop when you retire. In fact, it becomes even more vicious, because you're probably on a fixed income by this time. Thus, the need for inflation protection is an essential consideration when choosing long-term investments. Since you know that inflation has averaged three percent per year since 1916, it makes sense that you should plan to have your income increase by at least three percent per year during your retirement.

Will Your Money Last?

We have already seen how longevity can become a major risk factor in your retirement plan. Inflation risk goes hand in hand with longevity risk, because the longer you live, the more time there is for inflation to decimate your savings. Remember, at an average inflation rate of three percent, if you require $50,000 a year in today's dollars when you retire, you'll need $65,239 in 10 years' time, and $101,640 in 25 years.[5]

We have seen how you will need increasing amounts of retirement income just to keep pace with a three percent inflation rate. But that's not the whole story. You cannot tell for sure to what degree your retirement income needs will need to keep up with inflation. You may even be thinking that your income needs could decline in real terms if you become less active as you grow older and perhaps travel less. On the other hand, during your retirement years you are more likely to have more expensive costs such as healthcare, currently rising much faster than the average inflation rate. To illustrate this chilling thought, the U.S. Bureau of Labor Statistics developed an experimental inflation index called the CPI-E, which measured price changes for expenditures of people aged 62 and older. Since 1982, inflation in the CPI-E has been higher every year than that of the other major indices used by the Department of Labor, such as the CPI-U (all urban consumers), and CPI-W (urban wage earners and clerical workers). The CPI-W happens to be the inflation rate used by Social Security.[6] But then, you weren't going to depend on that, were you?

---

[1] U.S. Postal Service
[2] 2005 Financial Retirement Fears, National Association for Variable Annuities, March 28, 2005.
[3] Ibbotson Associates, 2004.
[4] *Investopedia.com.*
[5] Source: Ibbotson Associates, 2004.
[6] Social Security Administration, www.ssa.org.

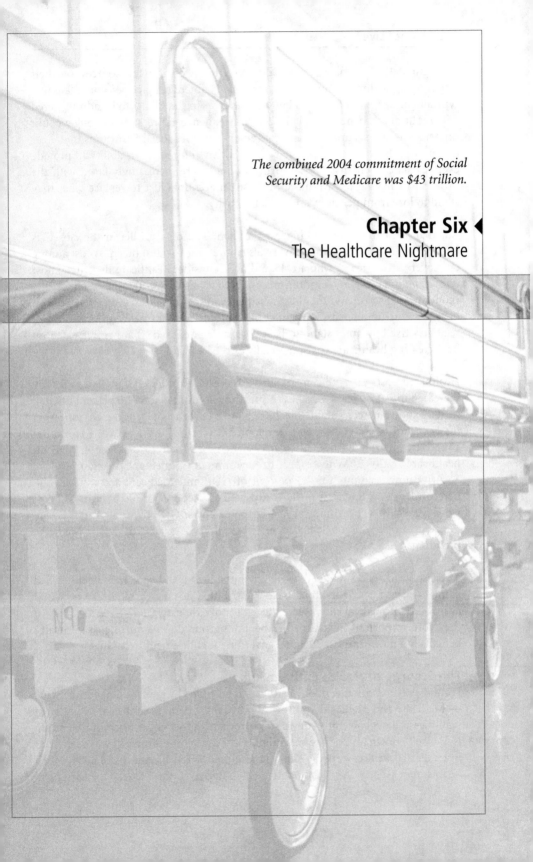

The combined 2004 commitment of Social Security and Medicare was $43 trillion.

Chapter Six ◀
The Healthcare Nightmare

Unfortunately, for many Baby Boomers, the two primary sources of their retirement income are in serious trouble. Defined benefit pension plans are typically under-funded or are being turned over to the PBGC to be administered with set limits on benefits paid out. As a consequence, retirees can no longer count on pensions as a secure source of retirement income. Social Security is in danger of running short of funds in a few years, which will reduce its ability to provide even legislated benefits. Thus, retiring Boomers are increasingly faced with the prospect of having to save more in personal accounts just to replace what they stand to lose from pensions and Social Security.

But that's not the Boomers' biggest problem. The real "gorilla in the closet" is healthcare. In fact, healthcare now rivals labor as the greatest business cost among employers.[1] Americans, who are 45 and over, consider healthcare the single most critical national issue — more important than terrorism/national security, the economy, education and the war in Iraq.[2] Given that increases in healthcare costs have far outrun increases in inflation, current and future retirees living on relatively fixed incomes stand to have a sizeable portion of that income eaten up by increasing healthcare costs, especially as retirees age.

Healthcare costs as a percent of gross domestic product (GDP) have steadily increased in recent years. U.S. health spending accounted for 14.6 percent of GDP in 2002 and 16 percent of GDP in 2004, almost twice as much as the Organization for Economic Cooperation and Development (OECD) average.[3] Only two other countries, Switzerland and Germany, spent more than 10 percent of GDP on healthcare in 2002.[4] With respect to government entitlement programs, Social Security now accounts for 4.3 percent of GDP and Medicare accounts for 2.6 percent. By 2079, Social Security is expected to account for 6.4 percent of GDP, while Medicare will account for nearly 14 percent of GDP by itself. And by 2030, 9.1 percent of a retiree's Social Security benefits will go toward paying Medicare premiums.[5]

These sobering percentages, of GDP attributable to healthcare, have been pushed along by several factors that have contributed to rising medical costs and availability of medical care. While the list is not exhaustive, let's consider a few of the more important factors before beginning our discussion of private health benefits, public health benefits and government entitlement programs.

The Scourge of Health Entitlements

For most retirees and the poor, healthcare is provided by government entitlements — Medicare and Medicaid, but the extent of the federal government's long-term liabilities and net commitments to such programs as Social Security and Medicare is not well known among the general public. These commitments have risen from just over $20 trillion in fiscal 2000 to more than $43 trillion in fiscal 2004. Much of this increase may be attributable to the passage of the Medicare prescription drug program, but continued increases in health commitments are likely to substantially increase with the retirement of the Baby Boomers. According to David M. Walker, comptroller general of the U.S., if we examine these commitments on a per-person or per-worker basis, the burden comes out to be more than $150,000 per American and $350,000 per full-time worker, up from $72,000 and $165,000 in 2000, respectively.[6]

These figures present a significant fiscal challenge. If a disciplined approach is not taken toward this challenge, lawmakers will likely pursue the traditional solutions: cut benefits, increase taxes or share a greater portion of the costs with beneficiaries. While all of these are likely options in the future to bring healthcare costs under control, they won't come near to closing the fiscal gap now facing Americans. Indeed, it is likely that retirees will face greater medical costs throughout their retirement years, costs that will continue to eat away at their limited income.

The Promises of Managed Care

Managed care, with its focus on preventative medicine, was supposed to revolutionize healthcare. By treating patients before they contracted illnesses and diseases, it might be possible to prevent or, get a head start on treatment before the illnesses became serious problems for patients. This prevention would reduce healthcare costs and reduce the number of medical facilities since the number of visits to treat serious illnesses would decrease. But preventative medicine hasn't worked out that way. Instead, we have more emergency room visits, fewer inpatient hospital beds, a shortage of nurses, an aging Baby Boomer population, increasing healthcare costs as a result of increased longevity, reduced access to insurance and a serious Medicare/Medicaid crisis.[7]

For instance, according to a 2004 report by the American Hospital Association, 48 percent of community hospitals reported that their emergency rooms were operating at overcapacity; this figure was 68 percent for urban hospitals. Nationally, emergency room visits have increased 23 percent since 1992 — 89.2 million visits in 1992 compared to 110.2 million in 2002.[8] As hospitals downsized and consolidated with the rise of managed care, the number of hospital beds declined. Since patients stayed fewer days, there was less need for hospital beds. In 1975, there were 942,000 beds; by 2003, that number had decreased to 813,000.[9] As the population continues to age and the need for medical facilities and care rises, the cost of medical care is increasing. In reality, managed care may have had the opposite of its intended effect. The coming issue for Baby Boomers is not financing their retirement income; it is financing their healthcare costs.[10]

No Insurance?

As incredible as it may seem in a country as rich as America, not everyone has health insurance. U.S. Census figures show that 45.8 million Americans — 15 percent of the total population — had no insurance in 2004, up from 45 million in 2003.[11] Twenty million American workers report having no health insurance, and in some states as many as 25 percent of workers go without health coverage. People who don't have insurance often pay more for health services, drugs and hospital visits. And if they don't pay, hospitals must either bear the costs of the service or pass them along to patients who are insured.[12] Since the uninsured and the under-insured are hospitalized 50 percent more often for problems that could have been prevented with routine treatment, they increase the pressure on medical facilities and medical costs.[13]

Data show that 41 percent of uninsured Americans report having difficulties setting appointments with doctors when they need to see one. Fifty-six percent of uninsured Americans have no personal physician or medical provider, and 20 percent report being in only poor to fair health.[14] Unquestionably, medical advances help us live longer lives, but only if we have access to medical care. And increasing medical costs are making access less of a sure thing, especially for the uninsured. Already, as many as 25 percent of Americans are cutting corners with medical care to avoid the higher costs.[15]

According to the Kaiser Commission on Medicaid and the Uninsured, 12 percent of children under 18 went without insurance at the beginning of 2005. That's nine million children.[16] These children, and many uninsured adults, might be covered by reallocating funds already earmarked for health insurance, but it would probably cause a taxpayer uproar since the whole process runs under the political radar.

For example, in 2006, the federal government expects to provide some $130 billion for Americans to buy health insurance. This is about 11 percent of all federal income tax revenue, and more than 20 percent of federal spending on Medicare and Medicaid. And the amount could grow as high as $180 billion by 2010. However, the money is not reaching many of the people who actually need it most, and funds are provided indirectly so that employers and workers receiving health insurance won't have to pay taxes on what it costs. According to President Bush's advisory panel on tax reform, about 50 percent of the tax breaks go to people who don't need them — those families making $75,000 or more a year. More than 25 percent goes to families making over $100,000. Consequently, we still have 18 percent of the population — adults and children — under age 65 who are uninsured.[17]

It's not just the uninsured feeling the brunt of higher healthcare costs. Sixty-two percent of the people who have insurance are struggling, which clearly points out the impact of higher premiums, deductibles and gaps in medical coverage. In 2004, 28 percent of insured families were unable to pay for some form of healthcare they received. And in that mass of middle-income, American families, 33 percent report not having enough money to pay medical costs in 2004, 31 percent report having paid at least $1,000 or more in out-of-pocket expenses, and 34 percent report having skipped medical treatment or filling a prescription because of higher costs.[18] This medical deficit is not likely to go away at any time soon; in fact, it will probably get worse.

A System Under Pressure

America's healthcare system stands in stark contrast to healthcare in most other developed countries. While most countries finance healthcare through taxes, the U.S. gets over 50 percent of its healthcare spending through private insurance plans — mostly from employers — and through individual out-of-pocket payments. The U.S. is the only industrialized democracy in the world without a complete, publicly funded, universal healthcare system.[19]

Healthcare in the U.S. is already under pressure from higher costs, and as Baby Boomers begin to retire, they will only add to the burden on healthcare in general and on Medicare in particular. Total expenditures on healthcare in America are expected to increase from just under $2 trillion a year now to as much as $3 trillion a year by the end of this decade.[20] Will the healthcare system be able to handle this increase? Let's examine these rising medical costs a bit closer.

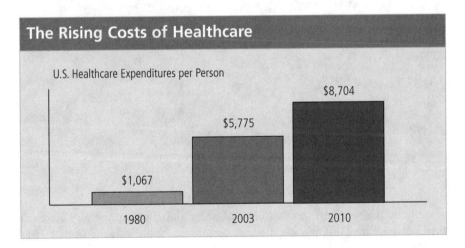

The Rising Costs of Healthcare

U.S. Healthcare Expenditures per Person

$8,704 — 2010
$5,775 — 2003
$1,067 — 1980

Escalating Costs

For most Americans, there is a growing uneasiness about rising healthcare costs. The increases are of such significance that they have begun to consume greater percentages of disposable income, causing decreases in consumer spending and saving. For instance, in 1980, healthcare expenditures per-capita were $1,067. By

2003, expenditures per person had risen to $5,775 — a five-fold increase over 1980. This expenditure is equivalent to 52 percent of the average retiree's Social Security income ($11,064).[21] By 2010, healthcare expenditures per capita are expected to rise to $8,704.[22]

Most Americans are accustomed to paying co-pays at least $20 per doctor's visit and anywhere from $15 on up for prescription drugs. These out-of-pocket costs are an added burden on people's income, especially as they age and move into retirement. Now more companies are moving toward a co-insurance model with their company-sponsored health plans. Workers, rather than paying co-pays, now pay a percentage of the medical bill. This co-insurance is often done to keep the premium prices lower, but the net effect is an increase in medical costs for workers and their families. For example, the average employee contribution to company-sponsored health insurance has increased more than 143 percent, and the average out-of-pocket payments for co-pays, deductibles and co-insurance rose 115 percent since 2000.[23]

Average Employee Healthcare Costs

Year	Average Employee Contribution	Average Out-of-Pocket Costs
2000	$662	$708
2001	$731	$689
2002	$877	$810
2003	$1,074	$980
2004	$1,284	$1,163
2005	$1,444	$1,366
2006*	$1,612	$1,524

*Projected amounts
Source: Hewitt Associates; Sandra Block, "Workers May Be in for Health Plan Sticker Shock," *USA Today*, October 20, 2005

A study by the Seattle firm of Milliman, Inc., a global consulting and actuarial firm, showed that the average medical cost for a family of four in 2005 was $12,214, an increase of 9.1 percent over 2004. The average rate of increase for this family over the four-year period between 2001 and 2005 was 9.8 percent per year. And the family would have paid out-of-pocket expenses of approximately $2,035 in 2005.[24]

According to the Employee Benefit Research Institute (EBRI) in Washington, D.C., healthcare costs are likely to rise higher and faster than most Americans anticipate. The EBRI estimates that such increases could add about 20 percent to the amount of pre-retirement income workers will need to replace in retirement.[25] One EBRI report conservatively estimates that a person retiring at age 65 in 2003 and living to age 80 would need to save $160,000 just to cover employment-based retiree health premiums and Medicare Part B premiums. If that same person lived to age 90, he or she would need to save $297,000 to cover these costs.[26] Yet, total household savings of 55- to 64- year-olds are estimated to be only $55,000.[27] This seems to suggest that Boomer retirement incomes may not be sufficient to support both an expected lifestyle and growing medical needs.

Serious Illnesses

Keeping up with increasing healthcare costs is tough enough, but when it involves a serious illness, the cost can be particularly catastrophic. A study by Harvard University researchers showed that medical costs were instrumental in the filing of nearly half of all personal bankruptcies in 2001. Approximately three-fourths of these bankruptcies were people who had basic health insurance when the serious illness struck, but during the illness many of them lost their insurance along with their job. For those whose illnesses resulted in filing bankruptcy, their out-of-pocket medical costs averaged $11,854. Those who battled cancer had much higher out-of-pocket expenses — an average of $35,878.[28]

A second fear arising from serious illness, beyond the mortality fear, is how the illness will affect the worker's job and, thus, access to health insurance. While sick workers have more legal safeguards today, and how workers are to be treated is broadly defined by legislation, the worker's actual treatment is determined by the workplace culture and the boss's sensitivity. Some companies bend over backward to help the worker maintain his or her job, while other companies adopt the attitude that everyone has problems—just do the job.[29]

Many healthcare observers fear that as insurance costs increase, companies may begin to make personnel decisions based on the cost of healthcare, even though legal constraints may prevent the application of any overt health criteria to job applications. In the past three years, healthcare costs have increased by double-digits. And if employers remain burdened with higher healthcare costs, they may lose their sensitivity toward the seriously ill and harden the environment in hopes that employees with health problems will give up and quit, taking their expensive illnesses along with them.[30]

Long-Term Healthcare

Most Americans believe they will live long, healthy lives, and will not be a burden to anyone. But 30 percent of the Medicare budget is spent on participants' last year of life, suggesting rapidly deteriorating health and high medical costs.

Daily Nursing Home Cost (Average for Private Room Per Day)			
Most Expensive Markets		**Least Expensive Markets**	
Statewide, AK	$531	Charleston, SC	$153
Stamford, CT	$348	St. Louis, MO	$148
San Francisco, CA	$330	Kansas City, MO	$146
New York, NY	$320	Tulsa, OK	$146
Hartford, CT	$292	Okla. City, OK	$141
Worcester, MA	$287	Wichita, KS	$139
Boston, MA	$277	Little Rock, AR	$137
Washington, DC	$271	Birmingham, AL	$135
Rochester, NY	$269	New Orleans, LA	$118
Honolulu, HI	$262	Shreveport, LA	$115

Source: MetLife Mature Market Institute, 2005

The average stay in a nursing home varies, of course, with a person's illness, medical condition and general state of health. For instance, people suffering from strokes spend an average of 61 months in care, those with cancer an average of 36 months in care and people suffering with Alzheimers will spend an average of 96 months in care.[31] If these patients have no long-term care (LTC) insurance, the cost of such care can be enormous. Most people don't buy LTC insurance because of other, more pressing expenses or needs. And many of them mistakenly believe that Medicare will cover those expenses. But family members of the elderly patient quickly find out that there is no Medicare coverage for long-term custodial nursing home care. If the elderly loved one is destitute, then they might qualify for some form of state-sponsored Medicaid assistance.[32]

A 2005 survey by MetLife's Mature Market Institute showed that average daily nursing home costs increased by 6 percent in 2005. The average daily cost for a private room was $203, up 5.7 percent from $192 in 2004. This brings the annual cost of a nursing home stay to $74,095, compared to just over $70,000 in 2004. Considering that the average nursing home stay is 2.4 years, the total average cost of the entire nursing home stay comes to approximately $177,828.[33] Clearly, more Boomers need to consider LTC insurance coverage while they are still relatively young and the insurance premiums are affordable. If they wait past age 60, LTC insurance may not be an affordable option.

According to the American Healthcare Association, nearly half of all Americans will need long-term care at some point in their life. But the insurance industry has had trouble selling LTC policies. In 2005, the industry sold just 326,000 policies valued at $700 million, down 25 percent from 2004. Yet the industry believes that as Boomers watch their own parents wrestle with long-term health issues, they will be more receptive to LTC insurance. Already, the average age of an LTC policyholder has fallen into the 50s from the high 60s and low 70s a decade ago.[34] And as Congress tightens the eligibility requirements for Medicaid coverage of nursing home care, more Boomers are likely to become interested in LTC insurance at an even earlier age.

Aside from nursing homes, many seniors find themselves in some other form of assisted living arrangement. According to a March 2005 report by the National Academy for State Health Policy, there are about 938,000 assisted-living residents in the U.S. This figure is, however, only an estimate since there is no standard definition of what assisted living means. The average annual cost of a one-bedroom assisted living facility increased by five percent in 2005 to an average of $30,300. But extra medical services such as blood tests, oxygen, rehabilitation services, etc., can add thousands of dollars to the total annual costs. These extra expenses must, of course, be covered out-of-pocket by the assisted-living resident.[35]

A growing segment of the long-term care industry is home healthcare. According to a report by the investment banking firm Cochran, Caronia & Co., revenues for home healthcare are likely to increase by as much as 15 percent annually over the next five years. The cost of a companion or caretaker — measured for the first time in 2005 — averaged $17 an hour. And a report from the Centers for Medicare and Medicaid Services suggests that national expenditures on home healthcare will reach $90 billion by 2014. Home healthcare was second in growth only to prescription drugs in 2003, and most observers believe that it will soon replace prescription drugs as the fastest growing cost area in the healthcare industry.[36]

Prescription Drugs

As just noted, prescription drug costs are the fastest growing costs in the healthcare industry. In 2004, the manufacturer's prices of the brand-name drugs most widely used by Americans rose by 7.1 percent, the highest growth rate in five years. This is over twice as much as the general 2.7 percent increase in the rate of inflation. On a per-prescription basis, patients paid an extra $51.56 more than in

2003, for the same prescription in 2004. So, if an elderly person were taking four prescriptions on a regular basis throughout the year, this person would pay $206.24 more for those prescriptions, if the patient had to pay the full price increase.[37]

For many retirees on fixed incomes, this represents a significant cost increase. And the cost of prescription drugs continues to grow. AARP reported that wholesale prices for the 200 brand-name drugs most commonly used by seniors — Americans over age 50 — increased an average of 6.1 percent during the 12 months ended in June 2005.[38] The new Medicare Part D plan for prescription drugs was supposed to help with increasing drug costs when it took effect January 1, 2006. However, it is still unclear whether seniors or retiring Boomers will actually see much savings from this plan.

Spending on specialty prescription drugs is growing twice as fast as for traditional prescription drugs. Specialty prescription drug sales reached $42 billion in 2004, and is expected to grow to around $69 billion in 2006. This category of drugs includes new medicines for cancer, rheumatoid arthritis and multiple sclerosis, among others.[39]

Employers and the government bear the majority of costs for these drugs, but they are asking patients to pick up more of the tab — as much as 50 percent. Treatments with these drugs can run from a few thousand dollars to as much as $600,000 per patient per year. According to the drug industry, such high costs are the result of developing the medicines and the expensive manufacturing processes for biotechnology medicines.[40] As more specialized medicines emerge for patient treatments, the costs of prescription medicines are likely to continue to lead the explosion in healthcare costs.

Private Sector Healthcare Benefits
Americans are beginning to learn something that Europeans have known for many years: If something is perceived as free, people will consume more than if they had to pay for it. The vast majority of healthcare costs for Americans are not paid directly by the users. Most of the costs are paid by a third party — either the government or an insurance company. Beneficiaries of this coverage are not strongly motivated to avoid unnecessary expenses or to shop for the best price when seeking medical care.[41] Given this fact, healthcare costs are very likely to continue to increase and will be a higher percentage of GDP in the next five to ten years — well beyond the 14 percent they now represent.

The private health insurance industry is marked by consolidation and heavy investing in technology and specialized programs, such as consumer-directed health plans. While some 2000 health insurers work in the industry, only five to ten companies dominate. The ten largest companies already control 48 percent of the insured population, up from 27 percent in 1995.[42] But the number of company-sponsored health insurance plans is in decline.

Declining Coverage

From 1993 to 2003, the number of large companies offering medical coverage to retirees dropped by approximately half, from 40 percent to 21 percent.[43] Experts expect this trend to continue, so retirees may not be able to count on retirement healthcare coverage from their employers. This lack will put an increasing burden on Medicare and the individual retiree.

In 1988, 66 percent of big firms' healthcare budgets went to cover retired employees. In 2005, only about 33 percent was designated for retiree coverage. But it's not just retirees who are feeling hard hit.[44] The portion of employers offering healthcare insurance to workers has fallen substantially in the last five years, dropping to 60 percent in 2005 from 69 percent in 2000. Small businesses are leading the coverage decline, declining from 68 percent coverage in 2000 to only 59 percent in 2005.[45] This decline has forced many individuals to search the market for individual insurance coverage.

Individual Insurance Coverage

The private, individual insurance option is usually the last resort for the roughly 60 million Americans who don't have health insurance coverage from their jobs or the government. This may not be a huge problem for most of these individuals. But for the approximately 17 million people, or 10 percent of Americans under age 65, who seek High Risk insurance through individual policies, finding coverage may be plagued with problems.[46] For example, severe medical illnesses such as cancer, diabetes, heart disease and HIV are barriers to insurance coverage. Such sick people often can't get insurance, and if they do, it is usually prohibitively expensive. And even if they can get insurance, it doesn't mean that all medical treatments will be covered. State insurance rules and the policy's fine print need to be carefully examined.

According to a RAND Corp. and the California Healthcare Foundation study, about 20 percent of non-elderly Americans aren't eligible for either employer plans or public health coverage. Denial rates on the individual insurance market range from eight to 18 percent. For instance, PacifiCare says that it approves individual policies for about 70 percent of its applicants without restrictions. It approves another 10 to 20 percent with restrictions — usually refusing to cover an existing health condition for a period of time. For the other 10 to 20 percent, it denies coverage. The company reasons: If too many sick people were insured without restrictions, premiums would be high for everyone and healthy people would not buy coverage.[47]

Benefit Comparison			
	General Motors UAW	General Motors White Collar PPO	Large Firm
Monthly Employee-Paid Premium	$0	$75	$187
Annual Deductible	$0	$0	$500
Out-of-Pocket Maximum	$250	$1,300	$1,000
Office Visit Co-Pay or Co-insurance	Full Amount	25%	$15/Visit
Hospitalization and Out-Patient Co-Pay	$0	$0	$15/Visit
Generic Retail Prescription Drugs	$5	$5	$20

Source: Julie Appleby and Sharon Silke Carty, "Ailing GM Looks to Scale Back Generous Health Benefits," *USA Today*, June 22, 2005

Unfortunately, people are most likely to purchase health insurance when they need it most or suspect that they will need it. This either increases the cost of the policy's premiums, or makes it easier for the insurance company to be selective and deny coverage.

Employer Insurance Coverage

For most Americans, health insurance coverage through an employer is a desirable situation. In a group policy situation, everyone must be covered under federal law. This spreads the risks among a larger number of people — reducing the premiums for everyone, at least in theory. But health insurance premiums and costs have increased significantly in recent years to the point that even employers are looking for ways to cut their health benefit costs. In addition, some employers find themselves having to absorb a larger portion of their employee's healthcare costs because of the promises and concessions they have made in the form of legacy benefits to unions. Consider, for example, the difference in what GM pays versus a large firm in the accompanying table. At present, employers are either decreasing their plan's coverage or passing along premium increases to their employees.

Limited Coverage

Today, about 16 million people pay for limited medical coverage, which puts them in the same medical boat as the under-insured — people who spend about five to

10 percent of their income on out-of-pocket medical expenses. Health insurance premiums rose 11.4 percent in 2004, several times the rate of inflation. As employers wrestle with these costs, they are passing a greater portion of the medical costs along to their employees. The typical change involves offering more limited plans or more expensive plans to employees. This increases the financial burden on employees. For instance, of those with limited coverage plans, 46 percent were contacted by collection agencies concerning unpaid medical bills. Thirty-eight percent did not fill some prescriptions because of their costs.[48]

Increasing Premiums

Annual health premium growth averaged 9.2 percent in 2005, down from 11.4 percent in 2004 and 13.9 percent in 2003. Yet, this increase was still three times the growth in worker's earnings and two-and-a-half times the rate of inflation, which now stands at 3.5 percent. Since 2000, health premiums have increased by 73 percent.[49]

Families are paying $1,094 more on average for their share of an employer's health insurance premiums than they did a year ago. In 2005, the total family premium cost surpassed the gross earnings for a full-time minimum-wage worker — $10,979 vs. $10,712. Overall, the expected underlying healthcare costs will be about 10 percent higher in 2006.[50]

Caring for the uninsured has also added to health insurance premiums. Families and employers paid an extra $922 on average in 2005 to cover the costs of caring for the uninsured. By 2010, these additional costs will be $1,502, and the total premium costs will hit $17,272. In at least 11 states, the costs of the uninsured will likely exceed $2,000 per family. And the costs also impacted single individuals covered by employer plans — $341 in 2005, and $532 in 2010. Total premium charges for individuals were $4,065 in 2005, and $6,115 in 2010.[51] And it's not just the private sector that is feeling the effects of these increases. Public health plans may, in some ways, be worse off.

Public Sector Healthcare Benefits

Current entitlement programs at the local, state and federal government levels may have already promised the next generation of retirees more in real resources than they will be able to deliver. The ever present slowing rate of labor growth compared to the increasing growth of retirees and rising healthcare costs makes additional current and future promises risky at best. As long as healthcare costs continue to grow faster than GDP, worker earnings and inflation, state and federal spending on health and retirement programs will send budgets out of control and rack up huge deficits that can't easily be paid.[52]

Over the next few years, state and local governments face an exploding budget problem. Unlike the private sector, 48 of the 50 state governments and more than half of all municipalities still provide healthcare benefits for workers after retirement. But lawmakers haven't bothered to set aside enough money to pay for these contractually guaranteed payments.[53] Cutting benefits to save money on future obligations is not a likely option since most public sector employees are represented by strong unions that would oppose such changes.

At present, public accounts reflect only the current healthcare expenditures, and that has generally been what was reported as the governments' obligation. The cost of future promises made by governments has not been recorded nor included in figuring healthcare obligations. Consequently, few people actually understand the true promised obligations that governments are really responsible for.[54] In the absence of an assessment of the real obligations to retirees, governments continue to make promises that they may not be able to keep in the future.

An accounting change scheduled to take effect by 2008 will force state and local governments to face up to the fact that they have made financial promises without planning for how these promises will be paid.[55] This change could have a significant impact on the public sector since benefits for workers tend to be more generous. Mercer Consulting estimates that governments that have not set aside money for future obligations may face liabilities 40 to 60 times more than the present annual cost of their retiree's healthcare. Compounding this problem is the fact that public sector workers are usually eligible for retirement earlier — mid 50s — than are private sector workers. This means they will probably collect benefits over a longer time period, costing governments even more money.

Surveying the Damage

Some states have already begun to assess the damage by examining their future long-term obligations. In October 2005, Maryland revealed a retiree healthcare liability of $20 billion, which will necessitate putting aside $1.6 billion annually to fund the liability. That's approximately 13 percent of the state's $12 billion budget, and comes on top of the $770 million already paid out for current employee and retiree healthcare benefits. North Carolina estimates its obligation at $13 to $14 billion, and some observers believe that California's obligation could run $40 billion or more.[56]

An increasing concern being voiced among the middle class about paying for public sector retirees' medical care has prompted several states to consider ways to extend health insurance to everyone. According to the National Conference of State Legislatures, lawmakers in about 19 states considered proposals to expand healthcare coverage in 2005.[57] In April 2006, lawmakers in Massachusetts approved a bill that would make their state the first to require residents who can't qualify for health coverage, at work or under Medicaid, to buy their own insurance.[58]

Estimates suggest that 22 states, both Democratic and Republican, will expand the eligibility for Medicaid programs in 2006. But another 14 states — slammed by rising healthcare costs — may scale back their Medicaid programs. For example, Tennessee has already cut 200,000 from its Medicaid rolls, and Missouri has cut another 100,000 residents from its rolls.[59]

Healthcare Entitlements

In addition to Social Security and health insurance plans for government employees, the federal government has two other entitlement programs — Medicare and Medicaid. The costs of the Medicaid program are shared with state governments, but the federal government pays about 59 percent of its costs. These two programs pose a significant threat to the American taxpayer. Both plans are financed by tax revenues, and they are the fastest growing of all the government's social programs. And according to the U.S. Census Bureau, Social Security, Medicare and Medicaid accounted for more than $1 trillion of the $2.2 trillion the federal government spent in 2004.[60]

Without our knowing it, the medical care programs paid by federal and state taxpayers have grown beyond what the average American could imagine. Today, about 100 million people — one in three Americans — now have government coverage through Medicare, Medicaid, the military and federal employee health plans. Another 10 million Americans are eligible for Medicaid benefits, but they haven't signed up for them. According to the U.S. Census Bureau, the median household income in 2003 was $43,318. Right now, a family of four, in most states, making $40,000 annually can get government health insurance for their children.[61] Increasingly, the government and the American taxpayer have taken on the responsibility of insuring the health coverage of seniors and low-income workers.

Medicare

Medicare is a federal health insurance program that covers about 43 million senior and disabled Americans. A person becomes eligible for Medicare by being disabled and collecting Social Security benefits or by reaching the age of 65. In 2004, Medicare had a negative cash flow. It consumes a large chunk of the overall federal budget, and it is a major contributor to the developing problem of funding healthcare in the U.S.

On January 1, 2006, Medicare Part D, the new prescription drug program, took effect. As a consequence, Americans 65 and older will likely spend a large and growing portion of their Social Security income on Medicare premiums and healthcare expenses. For example, a typical 65-year-old can expect to spend 37 percent of his or her Social Security income on Medicare premiums, co-payments and out-of-pocket costs in 2006. The percentage of Social Security devoted to healthcare is expected to increase to almost 40 percent in 2010, and to nearly 50 percent in 2021.[62] Since these healthcare expenses grow faster than inflation, seniors will really experience a reduction in benefits, evidenced by a lower usable income.

If we look at actual dollar amounts, seniors will likely pay $120 more a month for basic Medicare and the prescription drug plan in 2006. Many of these seniors can also plan on paying $100 to $200 more on supplemental Medigap policies — insurance needed to cover medical costs not covered by Medicare. This represents a substantial increase in health costs for seniors living on a small pension and Social Security income. A 2004 Urban Institute report estimated that Medicare premiums alone will rise to nearly 25 percent of the total Social Security income in 2040. Add to this Medigap premiums, and many Boomers could spend as much as 40 percent of their retirement income on healthcare.[63]

According to the Medicare trustees, Medicare Part A, which pays for hospital care, has an unfunded liability of $9.4 trillion for current participants, and a $14.7 trillion liability for future participants — a total of $24.1 trillion. Medicare Part B, which covers doctor visits, is unfunded by $25.8 trillion, even with the modest premiums paid by participants. Finally, Medicare Part D, the new prescription-drug program, will need $18.2 trillion from taxpayers to supplement beneficiary premiums and state transfers. The total of Medicare's unfunded liabilities comes to $68.1 trillion — six times Social Security's unfunded liability. Virtually 100 percent of all federal taxes, at present value, will be required to pay for just Social Security and Medicare.[64]

Medicare Part D is supposed to reduce the cost of prescription drugs to retired seniors. For the first time under any of Medicare's programs, the government asked the private sector to prepare plan packages for seniors to consider. Some 50 private insurance companies have developed dozens of prescription drug plans for Medicare participants, ranging from low- to high-level premiums. But there is a lot of uncertainty and confusion concerning what plan to purchase, what the plans cover, and how much it will cost as seniors start enrolling in the program. A *USA Today/CNN* Poll showed that only 37 percent of the seniors surveyed felt they understood the program at least somewhat well; 61 percent did not.[65]

> *"I have a Ph.D., and it's too complicated to suit me."*
> — William Q. Beard, 73, Retired chemist, Wichita, Kansas, referring to the Medicare drug plan. Source: Robert Pear, "Confusion Is Rife About Drug Plan as Sign-up Nears," *The New York Times,* Nov. 13, 2005

Congress, in writing the program, left some strange gaps that could end up costing retired seniors more money for their prescription drugs. For example, a low-premium plan would have a $250 annual deductible. Once the deductible is met, seniors would pay 25 percent of the drug costs until their total prescription costs reached $2,250. Then comes the "doughnut hole." At this point, coverage ends and retired seniors must pay for their medicine themselves. When they have spent $5,100, coverage resumes again with Medicare picking up 95 percent of prescription costs for the rest of the plan period.[66] The doughnut hole can be closed, but it requires prescription drug plans with higher premiums. For example, in Maryland, the monthly premium for one plan is $6.44. If one wants to plug the "hole," the premium jumps to $52.88 a month.[67] So the question really comes down to whether a retiree wants to spend more on the prescriptions or on the policy premiums. And as most critics of the program are quick to point out, the prescription-drug programs will add to the federal budget deficit for years to come.

When the prescription drug program went into effect, the system was not ready to handle the onslaught of seniors trying to fill their prescriptions. In some cases, pharmacies ended up paying the cost of drugs because Medicare had no record of the senior being signed up for the program. States overspent on prescription drugs for Medicaid patients who had been switched to Medicare for the drug program, and their records had not yet been updated so that Medicare could pay. It took over a month for the program to work out the kinks, and for the federal government to begin paying its obligation under the new program. Many seniors expecting to pick up their monthly supply of drugs were turned away and told they had no coverage.

As of April 2006, nearly 20 million people were enrolled in the drug benefit program, but only 3.6 million of these signed up voluntarily.[68] Many seniors have weighed the plans available to them and decided they would end up paying more for prescription drugs under the program than they were currently paying, especially when monthly premiums and co-payments were added into the costs. Their premiums will increase by one percent a month for every month they weren't enrolled in the program. So, if they wait a year to enroll, their premiums will be 12 percent higher.[69]

The U.S. government spent approximately $332 billion on Medicare in 2005. Over the coming decades, as Boomers retire and begin to demand better healthcare, which usually means expensive technology, Medicare threatens to bankrupt the federal government. Spending on the program will almost certainly grow to about 10 percent of GDP, about four times what it is now.

Medicaid

Medicaid provides health coverage for the poor. It gives them access to basic medical coverage. Medicaid is funded by state and federal tax revenues and the program is administered by the states.

Several years ago, the nation underwent welfare reform. It was very successful in moving people off cash assistance programs into low-paying jobs. But it created a group of people who no longer had access to affordable healthcare. Medicaid was expanded to cover these working poor. This expansion has put an enormous strain on federal and state finances that cover Medicaid costs, and it has made taxpayers the health insurance provider for millions of workers at Wal-Mart, McDonald's and other low-wage employers. It is, in fact, one step removed from a national healthcare system run by the federal and state governments.[70]

Medicaid Expenditures	
Year	Billions $
1990	$74
1997	$159
2004	$305
2005	$316.2

Growth in Medicaid spending has averaged 10 percent a year since 2000. It now totals over $300 billion a year, and spending over the next five years is expected to grow from 7 to 9 percent annually. As can be seen in the accompanying table, between 1990 and 2004, Medicaid expenditures increased by 85 percent, almost twice as much as spending on Medicare.[71]

Much of the growth in spending on Medicaid is attributable to the growth in enrollment. Between 1990 and 2004, Medicaid coverage grew from 23 million people to 41 million people. Current estimates place coverage at 53 million low-income and disabled Americans. The U.S. and state governments spend more on healthcare for this group of people than the British government spends on healthcare for its entire population of 60 million people.[72] These skyrocketing costs and swelling membership rolls have put Medicaid at the front of America's entitlement agenda. Medicaid has now passed K–12 education as the single largest expenditure item on most states' budgets.[73]

The problem has become so large that state governors and state legislatures are developing proposals for change in their Medicaid obligations. These obligations are huge. For example, *The McKinsey Quarterly* estimates that even after economic growth has leveled out, the Medicaid health insurance program will consume more than 75 percent of all new state revenue in at least ten states; from 50 to 75 percent of new revenue in 11 other states; and from 25 to 50 percent in 22 other states by the year 2009. At present, Medicaid represents 21 percent of state budgets, up from 13 percent a decade ago. And by 2009, the costs of Medicaid will rise to approximately 26 percent of state spending.[74] It's little wonder that states are seeking to have Medicaid recipients pay more of their medical care and to set limits on the scope of services provided.

Part of the problem with Medicaid may also be poor state controls on claims and a high level of fraud within many state systems. For instance, New York's Medicaid program is the most costly and most generous in the U.S. It now spends $44.5 billion annually on Medicaid. California covers 55 percent more people, but spends less than New York. New York spends an average of $10,600 for each of its 4.2 million Medicaid recipients — twice the national average. And according to the Government Accounting Office (GAO), as many as 40 percent of New York's Medicaid claims are questionable with respect to their validity. In fact, the GAO estimates that 10 percent of all national healthcare spending may be lost to fraud and abuse of the system.[75]

Clearly, the nation faces significant issues with its two health entitlement programs, and there are critical problems with private sector healthcare coverage. If changes aren't made, taxpayers face an ever-increasing tax burden to cover the costs of Medicaid and Medicare. Most attempts at reform or program changes in both the private and public sectors are aimed at passing a greater burden for healthcare cost on to the individual. For instance, private companies are considering shifting to a model of consumer-driven healthcare, which shifts more of the burden of costs and responsibility of healthcare to health plan participants — employees. (See the accompanying table for alternative ideas.) However, the grand plan still leaves a bit to be desired for retirees and workers.

Plans to Increase Participant Costs

• *Higher co-payments for office visits, prescription drugs, specialty care and emergency room visits.*

• *Reductions in retiree health plan coverage.*

• *Cap on beneficiary healthcare spending.*

• *Cutting medical benefits for plan participants.*

• *Health Savings Accounts (HSA) – Offers the participant tax breaks; requires employer to offer high-deductible health insurance plans; participant has control over assets.*

• *Health Retirement Accounts (HRA) – Offers participants lower tax breaks than HSA; employers control accounts and provide either high- or low-deductible health insurance plans; employer provides all account contributions.*

• *Section 125 Plans (FSA) – Offers participant some tax breaks; coordinates with all types of health insurance plans; contributions must be used by the plan year's end.*

• *Total Compensation Plan – Employees receive a single compensation amount over which they have total control to allocate among take-home pay, health benefits, retirement or savings plans, or non-health benefits.*

According to an EBRI/Commonwealth Fund survey, only 42 percent of respondents with consumer-driven health plans are satisfied with their plans and their insurance, compared to 63 percent who are pleased with their traditional plan coverage. Employees with consumer-driven plans are also less satisfied with both their choice of

"Many retirees now find they need 100 percent or more of pre-retirement income due to higher-than-anticipated healthcare costs."
— Karin Landry, Managing Partner, Spring Consulting Group, Boston

doctors and the quality of care than those with traditional coverage. This is where the new plans were supposed to excel, but it turns out that most of us do very little to find quality medical care or search for a lower-cost alternative.[76] Yet more of the costs of medical care will continue to be passed on to us — the individual consumer.

For retired seniors and soon-to-retire Boomers, the relevant question is "how much of an additional financial burden can we handle?" For many, the answer may be very little, given their limited retirement assets and incomes.

Cecil and Myrtle Glover

Cecil and Myrtle Glover lived in Vienna, a small rural town in Southern Illinois. Mr. Glover worked for over 40 years for Beamer Handle Company located in Southeast Missouri. He bought timber and sawed it into staves that could be made into hammer handles, pick handles, shovel handles, baseball bats, etc. Mr. Glover was also a Baptist Minister and pastored numerous churches, on weekends, throughout his life. Neither of his employers had pension plans or defined contribution plans. And he was never able to put away much in the way of savings while raising two children on a low-wage salary. Mrs. Glover worked sparingly — only when there was a pressing financial need. All the couple had to look forward to at retirement was Social Security.

Mr. Glover never fully retired. He began drawing his Social Security at age 65, but he continued to work for the handle company three days a week. He died of a massive heart attack in January 1987 at the age of 78. Upon his death, Mrs. Glover continued to collect survivor benefits from Social Security. She sold their house in the country and bought a trailer home in town to be close to people in case she ever needed help. At the time, she was 76 years old. The money left after purchasing the trailer home went into her checking account.

Mrs. Glover lived in the trailer home until she became so frail that her children — a son and a daughter — decided it was not safe for her to live alone any longer. A knee replacement surgery had made it difficult for her to get around well. In addition, she had broken her right arm in a fall and it would not heal because of her soft, porous bones. This made it difficult to use the arm, which limited what she could do for herself. She had made it clear that she did not want to live with her children, so the decision was made to put her in the local nursing home.

It was then that the family found out that Medicare would not cover any of the costs of the nursing home care. In Illinois, Medicaid would have covered the nursing home care but for one small problem — Mrs. Glover had not divested herself of her assets three years before entering the nursing home. Only when her assets were depleted to $2,000 would Medicaid start to pay the expenses.

Mrs. Glover entered the nursing home in January 2003. When she entered the nursing home, she had a certificate of deposit worth $25,000, a checking account with about $15,000 and $15,500 in assets from the sale of her trailer home. Her monthly Social Security benefit was about $1,200. She had total assets of $55,500.

Mrs. Glover paid $87 a day for a semi-private room in the nursing home. This included her lodging, food and 24-hour-a-day care. The monthly total was about $2,697. Her medicines were extra out-of-pocket costs, as were incidentals needed to keep her comfortable. Her $1,200 Social Security check went toward paying her monthly nursing home costs, with the remaining $1,497 coming out of her assets. Her medicines and incidentals ran around $1,000 per month. Overall costs for the nursing home stay per month were $3,697.

Mrs. Glover died in May 2004, two months from her 92nd birthday. Her 17-month nursing home stay had cost $62,849, $42,449 of which came directly out of her available assets. The other $20,400 came from her Social Security checks. Her family was left with approximately $13,000 in assets after her death. If she had lived another five months, Medicaid would have taken over her nursing home expenses, including her medicines.

---

[1] "Healthcare Is Biggest Business Cost Concern, New Buck Consultants Survey Finds," *Mellon.com*, September 7, 2005.

[2] Employee Benefit Research Institute and Matthew Greenwald and Associates, 2005.

[3] "Desperate Measures," *The Economist*, January 28, 2006.

[4] "Prices Drive Up Health Costs in U.S. – Study," *Insurance Newscast*, July 13, 2005.

[5] Greg Crawford and Vineeta Anand, "Retirement Disaster: Defining the 3 Legs of the Stool . . . or Should it Be 4?" *Pensions & Investments*, April 18, 2005.

[6] David M. Walker, "Spending Is Out of Control," *BusinessWeek*, November 14, 2005.

[7] Edward J. Crowder, "Emergency Rooms Jammed," *Connecticut Post*, May 1, 2005.

[8] Ibid.

[9] Ibid.

[10] Crawford and Anand, op. cit.

[11] "Study: 20 Million U.S. Workers Lack Health Insurance," *Insurance Newscast*, April 29, 2005.

[12] Ibid.

[13] Crowder, op. cit.

[14] *Insurance Newscast*, op. cit.

[15] Julie Appleby, "Even the Insured Can Buckle Under Healthcare Costs," *USA Today*, August 30, 2005.

[16] John M. Broder, "Health Coverage of Young Widens With States' Aid," *The New York Times Online*, December 4, 2005.

[17] Eduardo Porter, "Healthcare for All, Just a (Big) Step Away," *The New York Times Online*, December 18, 2005.

[18] Appleby, op. cit.

[19] "Headaches for All," *The Economist.com*, October 7, 2005.

[20] Ibid.

[21] Social Security Administration, 2004.

[22] National Center for Health Statistics, 2004.

[23] Sandra Block, "Workers May Be in for Health Plan Sticker Shock," *USA Today*, October 20, 2005.

[24] "Milliman Says Annual Medical Cost for 'American Family of Four' is $12,214," *Insurance Newscast*, May 27, 2005.

[25] Ron Panko, "Security Gap," *Best's Review* (October 2005).

[26] Paul Fronstin and Dallas Salisbury, "Retiree Health Benefits: Savings Needed to Fund Healthcare in Retirement," Employee Benefit Research Institute Issue Brief No. 254 (February 2003). Assumes a 14% annual increase in healthcare premiums, and a 4% after-tax rate of return on invested assets. Retiree pays 100% of group market insurance premium, $1,500 maximum out-of-pocket expenses and Medicare Part B premiums.

[27] Congressional Research Service. 2004. Assumes 3% rate of inflation.

[28] Kelly K. Spors, "Serious Illness, Serious Bills," *The Wall Street Journal Online*, October 10, 2005.

[29] Lisa Belkin, "Sick and Vulnerable, Workers Fear for Health and Their Jobs," *The New York Times Online*, December 17, 2005.

[30] Ibid.

[31] Sue Stevens, "The Ins and Outs of Long-Term Care Insurance," *Morningstar.com*, September 29, 2005.

[32] Jerald Winakur, "What Are We Going to Do With Dad?" *Washingtonpost.com*, August 7, 2005.

[33] Trevor Thomas, "Average Annual Nursing Home Cost Hits $74,000, Survey Finds," *National Underwriter Life & Health*, October 3, 2005.

[34] Jeff D. Opdyke, "Insurers Push Policies for Long-Term Care," *The Wall Street Journal Online*, December 27, 2005.

[35] Ellen Hoffman, "A Careful Checkup for Assisted Living," *BusinessWeek Online*, June 3, 2005.

[36] "Home Healthcare Poised for Future Market Growth; Industry Trends Drive Sustainable Revenue Growth of up to 15 Percent," *Insurance Newscast*, October 13, 2005.

[37] Kristen Gerencher, "AARP: Drug Prices Jump 7.1% in 2004," *MarketWatch*, April 13, 2005.

[38] Julie Appleby, "AARP: Drug Prices Zoom Past Inflation," *USA Today*, November 2, 2005.

[39] Getta Anand, "As Biotech Drug Prices Surge, U.S. Is Hunting for a Solution," *The Wall Street Journal Online*, December 28, 2005.

[40] Ibid.

[41] Michael Tanner, "A Hard Lesson About Socialized Medicine," *cato.org*, September 23, 1996.

[42] Sandra Ward, "WellPoint's Advantage," *Barron's Online*, July 25, 2005.

[43] Janice Revell, "Healthcare Crisis: The Great State Healthcare Giveaway," *Fortune*, April 19, 2005.

[44] "Clearly Unhealthy," *The Economist*, July 2, 2005.

[45] Kristen Gerencher, "Health Premiums up 9.2% This Year," *MarketWatch*, September 14, 2005.

[46] Sarah Lueck, "Seeking Insurance, Individuals Face Many Obstacles," *The Wall Street Journal Online*, May 31, 2005.

[47] Ibid.

[48] "Limited Medical Insurance Not Much Help — Study," *Insurance Newscast*, June 16, 2005.

[49] Gerencher, op. cit.

[50] Ibid.

[51] "Uninsured Add $900 to Health Premiums," *Insurance Newscast*, June 9, 2005.

[52] "Greenspan's Remarks Before the Joint Economic Committee, U.S. Congress," *The Wall Street Journal Online*, November 3, 2005.

[53] Revell, op. cit.

[54] "Clearly Unhealthy," op. cit.

[55] Deborah Solomon, "State, Local Officials Face Looming Healthcare Tab," *The Wall Street Journal Online*, November 23, 2005.

[56] Ibid.

[57] Julie Appleby, "States Take Healthcare Problem in Own Hands," *USA Today*, November 8, 2005.

[58] Barbara Chai, "Massachusetts Takes Big Step Toward Universal Healthcare," *The Wall Street Journal*, April 5, 2006.

[59] Ibid.

[60] "U.S. Census Bureau Tip Sheet: Consolidated Federal Funds Report for Fiscal Year 2004," *U.S. Newswire*, December 27, 2005.

[61] Dennis Cauchon, "Workers Swelling Rolls of Medicaid," *USA Today*, August 2, 2005.

[62] William Welch, "Medical Costs Eat at Social Security," *USA Today Online*, September 13, 2004.

[63] Howard Gleckman, "Medicare's Big Experiment," *BusinessWeek*, October 10, 2005.

[64] Bruce Bartlett, "Medicare and Social Security's Unfunded Liabilities," National Center for Policy Analysis, April 27, 2005.

[65] Joseph Schuman, "Medicare Program Is Little Understood," The Morning Brief, *The Wall Street Journal Online*, October 4, 2005.

[66] Barbara Martinez and Sarah Lueck, "How to Choose a Medicare Drug Plan," *The Wall Street Journal Online*, October 4, 2005.

[67] "Medicare Surprise," *BusinessWeek Online*, May 1, 2006.

[68] Sarah Lueck and Vanessa Fuhrmans, "Large Insurers Are Big Winners In New Medicare Benefit," *The Wall Street Journal Online*, April 21, 2006.

[69] Karen DeMasters, "Clients Lost In Medicare Lurch," *Financial Advisor*, March 2006.

[70] Dennis Cauchon, "Welfare Reform Opens Medicaid to Millions," *USA Today*, August 1, 2005.

[71] Robert Pear, "States Propose Sweeping Changes to Trim Medicaid by Billions," *The New York Times Online*, May 9, 2005.

[72] Lenny T. Mendonca, Vivian E. Riefberg and Craig P. Tanio, "Intensive Care for Medicaid," *The McKinsey Quarterly* (January 2005).

[73] Kathleen Hunter, "Governors to Lobby for Medicaid Reforms," *SeniorJournal.com*, June 13, 2005.

[74] Lenny T. Mendonca, et. al., op. cit.

[75] Clifford J. Levy and Michael Luo, "New York Medicaid Fraud May Reach Into Billions," *The New York Times Online*, July 18, 2005.

[76] Howard Gleckman, "Healthcare Plans' Uncertain Prognosis," *BusinessWeek Online*, December 14, 2005.

60% of American adults have saved less than $10,000!

Chapter Seven ◄
Red, White and Broke

Let's say you are fortunate enough to accumulate enough money to overcome most of the challenges discussed in this book. Now comes the final challenge that investors can fall victim to: the errors they make in managing their retirement money.

"I'm not so concerned with the return on my money as I am with the return of my money."
— Will Rogers

Research shows that investors do not always follow a prudent retirement plan. After all the work involved in gaining a retirement nest egg, investors still risk their hard-won savings in many different ways. Consider the following:

- **Six out of ten do not have a retirement account**[1] — An astounding 60 percent of workers haven't started a retirement account. Getting started is the most important part of any plan.
- **Nine out of ten don't have a financial plan** — Ninety percent haven't taken the time to create a financial plan. The unfortunate fact is that most Americans probably spend more time planning for a vacation than they spend planning for retirement.
- **Six out of ten adults have saved less than $10,000**[2] — For those who have started saving, they have saved less than $10,000.

And there's evidence that those who actually have managed to accumulate a retirement portfolio have experienced disappointing results.

And it's no wonder. The fund trading scandals of recent years have depleted investor confidence. The bursting of the tech bubble, as well as the Enron and WorldCom debacles, have all contributed to investor fears. When investors are fearful, they may try to over-compensate in their pursuit of their financial goal — which makes them vulnerable to more mistakes.

Indeed, America has a serious problem, a problem exacerbated by the fact that many Americans just don't see the problem clearly. The problem is investor error. When it comes to how investors manage their money for retirement, they must face the reality that they may not be in the great position they think they are. They are subject to a variety of errors, misperceptions and costly blunders.

Americans' savings habits are poor and getting worse. The chart below shows just how dismal the savings situation is. It's time to reverse the trend and begin a systematic savings and investment program for financial security. A program that will protect you and your spouse's retirement without putting undue hardship on your family.

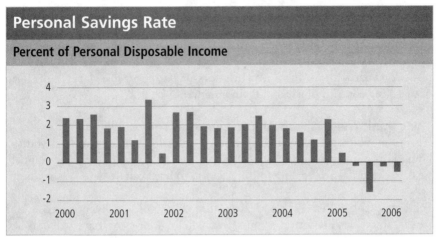

Source: U.S. Department of Commerce: Bureau of Economic Analysis

Common Investor Blunders
Almost any investment carries some risk. Investors, however, can complicate the risk factors by committing one or more errors when it comes to managing their portfolios.

Here are some of the most common — and most devastating — investor mistakes:

They Have No Retirement Account at All
Fifty-nine percent of workers do not have a retirement account.[3]

The Federal Reserve Board reports that more than half of non-retired adult Americans have either not begun saving or report having saved less than $10,000 for retirement; 36 percent have not begun to save for retirement and 16 percent have saved less than $10,000.

The biggest blunder anyone can make is to ignore their future by not saving for retirement. As more of the 77 million Baby Boomers move closer to retirement, many need to shift their thinking from "living for today" to saving for tomorrow. It's never too late to begin to save for the future. And doing so requires a plan.

They Have No Solid Retirement Plan
Even for those with an adequate retirement fund, the keys to retirement planning success are: making sure that they will have enough retirement income to supplement Social Security, and to help cover retirement expenses that last the duration of their retirement.

Only one in ten Americans has a written financial plan, yet overcoming their financial concerns tops the "wish lists" of the majority of adults nationwide, according to a national survey by American Express Financial Advisors.[4] A study by Hewitt Associates shows that three out of ten employees eligible for 401(k) plans don't participate. That means investors are *passing up free money* in the form of matching contributions from their employers.

They Think They Can Do All the Investing Themselves
History shows that do-it-yourself investors can be much like their do-it-yourself home improvement counterparts. The projects are frequently poorly planned, weak in execution and seldom finished. Do-it-yourself can be "wreck-it-yourself."

For example, between 1984 and 2002, the S&P 500 Index experienced a 12.2 percent increase; the average equity mutual fund investor returned only 2.6 percent during the same time period.[5]

Individual investors seldom have the discipline, patience or expertise to know where to place their investments. Like other facets of their lives, they need the advice of experts. This fact leads to the next investor blunder.

They Do Not Have an Expert Adviser
Nine out of ten Americans (87 percent) say they rely on others for financial advice, however, one's spouse or parents are most sought for that counsel. According to a 2005 Thrivent Financial survey of American adults — 31 percent of Americans say they primarily rely on a relative's advice about saving and investing money, while 27 percent consult a financial services professional, 16 percent consult a friend or co-worker, 8 percent rely on financial publications or television shows, 4 percent seek advice through the Internet, and 10 percent say they rely only on themselves.[6]

Are you really going to rely on advice from your uncle Marvin or the gals down at the bowling alley? For proper advice about your financial future you should seek the advice of proven professionals.

They Practice Irrational Behavior with Their Investments
Investors can be wild or timid, usually when the situation calls for the opposite behavior. They can be reckless in a bull market, or too fearful in a bear market. According to a Dalbar, Inc. 2005 study, investors are motivated by greed and fear — not sound investment practices. Close examination of investor behavior reveals that as markets rise, investors pour cash into mutual funds, and a selling frenzy begins after a decline. As markets rise, cash flows increase; as markets decline, the cash flows decline.

"Investors who change their investment approach — and shift assets as a result — based on the recent history in the capital markets are far more likely to do damage to their long-term financial well-being than those who follow a comprehensive financial plan," says Beverly Moore, managing director of wealth management at Mainstay. "We're seeing a real disconnect between investors' attitudes and their lifetime goals. They're driving by the rear-view mirror." [7]

They Save Too Little and Start Too Late

Even those Americans who do try to save, often commit a mistake when they set aside too little. In 1999, the national savings rate dipped below 3% for the first time since 1959, according to the U.S. Commerce Department. It has been declining further since then, and in 2005 it was negative (-0.5 percent), lagging behind nearly all other developed countries.

Many investors do not start a retirement savings program until they are in their 30s. However, money saved early and left to grow over a 40-year career will compound to a greater amount than those who try to play "catch up" later in life.

In this example, hypothetical investor Nick puts away just $1,000 per year for ten years ($10,000 total), between his 20th and 30th birthdays. He leaves the money alone until he reaches age 70. His sister, Nicole, is a late saver. She realizes she has to "catch up" to her brother, but doesn't start until she's 56. She invests $5,000 per year for fifteen years ($75,000). Despite investing over seven times what her brother did, at 7% interest her total fund at age 70 is about *$100,000 less than* Nick's fund!

They Don't Invest for the Long Run

Long-term planning means deflecting the inevitable damage done by inflation and unanticipated costs, such as medical and nursing home care. For example, according to Ibbotson, if you need $50,000 a year to live on today, assuming a three percent inflation rate, you'll need nearly double that amount — $100,000 — in 25 years just to maintain the same lifestyle.

American retirees in 2030 are projected to fall at least $45 billion short of covering basic expenditures and nursing home or home healthcare.[8] As part of any long-term investment plan, be sure to account for future healthcare premiums. Even new programs such as the Medicare prescription drug plan cover primarily low-income retirees relying almost exclusively on Social Security.

They Don't Diversify Their Assets

A study by Hewitt Associates demonstrates that despite horror stories about employees at scandal-scarred companies such as WorldCom and Enron having their 401(k) accounts wiped out because they had all their money riding on their own company's stock, 27 percent of 401(k) investors still have more than half of

But What If I Live?

Age	Nick's Contributions	Nick's Savings	Nicole's Contributions	Nicole's Savings
20	1,000	1,070.00	0	0.00
21	1,000	2,214.90	0	0.00
22	1,000	3,439.94	0	0.00
23	1,000	4,750.74	0	0.00
24	1,000	6,153.29	0	0.00
25	1,000	7,654.02	0	0.00
26	1,000	9,259.80	0	0.00
27	1,000	10,977.99	0	0.00
28	1,000	12,816.45	0	0.00
29	1,000	14,783.60	0	0.00
30	0	15,818.45	0	0.00
31	0	16,925.74	0	0.00
32	0	18,110.54	0	0.00
33	0	19,378.28	0	0.00
34	0	20,734.76	0	0.00
35	0	22,186.20	0	0.00
36	0	23,739.23	0	0.00
37	0	25,400.98	0	0.00
38	0	27,179.04	0	0.00
39	0	29,081.58	0	0.00
40	0	31,117.29	0	0.00
41	0	33,295.50	0	0.00
42	0	35,626.18	0	0.00
43	0	38,120.02	0	0.00
44	0	40,788.42	0	0.00
45	0	43,643.61	0	0.00
46	0	46,698.66	0	0.00
47	0	49,967.56	0	0.00
48	0	53,465.29	0	0.00
49	0	57,207.86	0	0.00
50	0	61,212.42	0	0.00
51	0	65,497.28	0	0.00
52	0	70,082.09	0	0.00
53	0	74,987.84	0	0.00
54	0	80,236.99	0	0.00
55	0	85,853.58	0	0.00
56	0	91,863.33	5,000	5,350.00
57	0	98,293.76	5,000	11,074.50
58	0	105,174.33	5,000	17,199.72
59	0	112,536.53	5,000	23,753.70
60	0	120,414.09	5,000	30,766.45
61	0	128,843.07	5,000	38,270.11
62	0	137,862.09	5,000	46,299.01
63	0	147,512.43	5,000	54,889.94
64	0	157,838.30	5,000	64,082.24
65	0	168,886.98	5,000	73,918.00
66	0	180,709.07	5,000	84,442.26
67	0	193,358.71	5,000	95,703.21
68	0	206,893.82	5,000	107,752.44
69	0	221,376.38	5,000	120,645.11
70	0	236,872.73	5,000	134,440.27
	10,000		75,000	

Does not include taxes.

their money in their employer's shares.[9] Many investors don't understand that most investments are not insured against loss. They need to understand that they could lose money with stocks, bonds or mutual funds. To fight this danger, diversifying their assets is the best defense.

They Carry a Large Amount of Debt into Retirement

Consumer debt reached $1.97 *trillion* as of June 2003; in 1981, it was at $378 *billion*.[10] Today's amount of consumer debt translates into approximately $18,700 per U.S. household. Outstanding consumer credit, including mortgage and other debt, reached $9.3 trillion in April 2003, an increase over the $7 trillion in January 2000. Total credit card debt alone stands at $735 billion; the household card debt of those carrying balances is estimated to average $12,000. Americans spent a near-record 18.1 percent of their after-tax income to cover their debts in 2004.

They Raid Their Retirement Funds Prematurely

A simple bit of advice: Don't do it. Don't even think about it. "Dipping," as it's called, can be the single worst thing a pre-retiree can do to sabotage a retirement fund, particularly 401(k)s and IRAs. Saving rates are already bad enough. Doing something that takes away from a growing retirement fund will lead directly to future misery. Not only is the money withdrawn taxable in the year taken, but it also makes a lower savings bottom line, which may be impossible to restore.

Investors are subject to a variety of blunders and errors, some of their own making, some inadvertent, but all preventable. Investing for retirement is difficult enough without falling into these traps. It's important to avoid these common mistakes in order to make your retirement as worry-free as possible.

Boomer Investors

Baby Boomers are in an especially vulnerable position. They are approaching retirement quickly and know they have under-saved and over-spent. They experienced the roaring 1990s with its dot com and tech boom. Then came the recession of 2000 — $7.7 trillion of paper wealth evaporated — that is still rippling through the economy today. The math is simple: Just a 50 percent loss wipes out a 100 percent gain.

With approximately 77 million people between the ages of 40 and 60, Baby Boomers represent the largest segment of today's U.S. population. Even though many of these Boomers plan to work beyond age 70, today's longevity trends clearly show that they could still spend another 10 to 20 years living in retirement. Research shows that Boomers typically underestimate the amount of income they will need in retirement, and not just by a little. Because of increasing life expectancy, retirees will likely need income from multiple sources, which are best managed in a comprehensive retirement plan.

Boomer Personality Types

Prudent *(20% of respondents). Have sound financial habits such as disciplined investing, ability to stick to a budget and monitor savings.*

Apprehensive *(27% of respondents). Know they are supposed to save for retirement, but their best results lag behind their goals. They are apprehensive about retirement.*

Optimistic *(19% of respondents). Are over age 45 and have saved less than $100K. Even with their paltry nest egg, 80% of this group isn't the least bit worried about financing their retirements.*

Worriers *(21% of respondents). Have good reason to worry. Engage in careless spending, often regret their purchases and spend money to make themselves feel better.*

Realists *(13% of respondents). Will need Social Security the most. Two-thirds think they have to work during their golden years, and more than 70% are apprehensive about retirement or downright dread it.*

But What If I Live?

A survey by Allstate Corp. suggests that a Boomer's personality type drives his/her retirement savings. For example, advisers who have clients who are optimists, worriers, or realists may need to spend extra time on their retirement plans. These personality types are the most resistant to implementing effective retirement strategies. And they make up over half of Boomer personality types.[11]

Boom or Bust? The Baby Boomers as Investors

The Baby Boomers have seen it all. In the early '70s it was inflation and the 1973 oil shock. Then it was more inflation and another oil shock in the late '70s. Then a booming market of the '80s, the short, mild recession of 1991 and another boom, this time the Internet bubble, came along in the late '90s. It all fell with a thud when the 1999-2001 stock market crash took down the high-flying, overconfident Boomers.

This generation has experienced record bull and bear markets in the same investing life cycle. It's a story wilder than fiction. This generation cut its investing teeth on one of the longest and greatest bull markets in modern history. Then they got caught in the fiercest bear market since the Great Depression — in many cases, wiping out virtually all of their gains.

And when the wild ups and downs were over, the Boomers emerged from the maelstrom, and they had all gotten a lot older. Twenty years after the wild ride of the '80s and '90s the same investors are now at the age where they are less tolerant of risk and more inclined to very conservative investing.

[1] Federal Reserve Board, 2004.

[2] *USA Today* (November 2005).

[3] *USA Today* (November 2003).

[4] "Need a Financial Adviser? Ask These Questions to Find Out." Mark McCrocklin. *The Times*, December 25, 2004.

[5] First Command Financial Planning, 2003.

[6] 2005 Thrivent Financial Survey.

[7] James J. Green, "Gen Xers May Make Better Clients," *Advisor.com*, September 16, 2005.

[8] "Want Fries With That, Sonny Boy?" *Motley Fool.*

[9] Adam Shell. "Most Americans No Good at Investing." *USA Today*, March 23, 2005.

[10] Federal Reserve Board.

[11] "Personality Drives Retirement Savings," *www.investmentnews.com*, November 14, 2005.

Chapter Eight ◀
It's Not Too Late

The American retirement crisis is here. Elements of the perfect storm — longevity, pensions, Social Security, high taxes, inflation, healthcare, and investor errors — have washed ashore. Now what? For Boomers who are about to retire or who are planning for it, the time has come to face the crisis and anticipate the inevitable fallout. It's not too late; there's still time for planning and saving. But you must begin now!

First and foremost, investing Boomers must be determined to *save rather than spend*. This probably means a change of mindset and spending habits and a modification of one's lifestyle. Such changes may be subtle or drastic, but they must be made. Saving should be part of a Boomer's routine — a part of everyday life.

Incorporating a savings mindset into your life makes it easier to embrace the second key part of the plan — *maximizing your annual savings for the future*. When saving is a habit, it takes less of a bite out of your lifestyle. By building savings into your routine, you are achieving goals for your entire life span — looking at the "big picture" instead of focusing shortsightedly on the next day, week or month.

A third key to a good retirement-oriented lifestyle is *focusing on long-term retirement needs*. Saving for retirement is a long-term proposition and requires commitment, consistency and perseverance. These qualities may help you with any of your goals or dreams, but they are especially important for the pursuit of a successful, comfortable retirement.

Finally, the fourth key part is to *get professional advice and follow it*. Most people cannot do everything by themselves. You probably do not do your own dentistry or fix your own computer. So why not use the help of a professional when it comes to investing for your retirement?

Preliminary Steps to Planning

Given the fact that most Boomers have done little in the way of planning for retirement, some preliminary steps may be a great place to begin. Start with baby steps if necessary, but start. If you are in the first wave of Boomers, you have less than ten years until you reach retirement age. If you are in the second wave, then you may have 20 years before reaching retirement age, but the sooner you begin, the more you will have in retirement.

Start Saving Immediately

As a first step, start saving immediately. You would be amazed at how large a nest egg you can build even in just ten years' time. If your company offers a 401(k) or some other retirement savings program, contribute the maximum amount to the plan. If you qualify for an IRA — either a traditional or a Roth — contribute as much as you can every year. And if you are 50 or older, take advantage of the senior catch-up contributions allowed by the IRS.

Disciplined saving for retirement is critical if aging Boomers are going to be prepared for retirement. Rather than hiding from the issue or believing that somehow the government or the tooth fairy will solve the problem, re-prioritize your needs and make retirement savings a primary concern.

Eliminate and Avoid Taking on Additional Debt

For Boomers still wanting to buy that dream home or the classic convertible they always wanted, if it means incurring additional debt that could be avoided, do not do it. If you are carrying significant debt such as credit card bills with double-digit interest rates that never seem to be paid off, incurring more debt on top of that is not only foolhardy, but a formula for financial disaster before and during retirement. If at all possible, paying off one's mortgage, car and credit card debt will only enhance retirement.

Possibly Postpone Retirement a Few Years

Postponing retirement may be advisable depending on what the Boomer has accumulated for retirement. For those individuals who hoped to retire at 55 with not a care in the world, that dream may not be possible if they do not have the assets accumulated to support their retirement. Boomers can't rely on Social Security to support their retirement. In fact, a 2005 study by the Center for Workforce Development at Rutgers University suggests that part of the retirement anxiety people feel comes from doubts about the soundness of government retirement programs. However, many pre-retirees have nothing to supplement their retirement income beyond Social Security benefits.[1]

Develop or Reassess Your Retirement Plan

If you are still trying to build your retirement portfolio, you may have to take on more risk in your investing. It is not recommended to have your entire stock portfolio tied up in one sector or in high-risk stocks, but investing a larger amount of money in stocks may be advisable. Make sure that the core of your stock holdings are in stable blue-chip companies, and consider adding an annuity if you are looking at investments with the benefit of tax-deferral.

It is possible to achieve a comfortable retirement by choosing a single investment or a small group of similar investments, but history shows that you can attain higher returns with lower risk through a strategy of asset allocation. This divides the money among a variety of different investments that collectively provides a mix of risk and return. These choices may not seem appropriate when considered individually, but together they offer a well-diversified portfolio.

Need for an Adviser-Client Relationship

Because you can't do all of your retirement plan yourself, the best course of action is to seek the advice of a skilled financial professional. With all the ups and downs of the market, most investors urgently need financial guidance. You most likely will need an adviser who:

- Understands the underlying reasons for a client's behavior and the types of investment mistakes they may have made in the past.
- Listens carefully to his or her clients and explains concepts and plans to them in a thoughtful and constructive way.
- Works closely to build the trust necessary for clients to move forward with the adviser's investment recommendations.

What to Look for in a Financial Adviser

It is extremely important to have a trustworthy, attentive financial adviser. Without saying whom you should hire, you should understand that surveys show the major reasons why people leave their financial adviser are: little or no regular contact; poor investment performance; a bad working relationship (poor "chemistry"); and poor customer service.

Investors should look for a qualified professional background for any potential financial adviser they are considering. The adviser should also have competent product knowledge, training — shown by the acquisition of investment industry designations, experience, attentive service — and quality performance. Do not be afraid to check references, business and industry bureaus, the Internet and other sources of information on someone you are about to trust with the bulk of your life savings.

Focus on Relationship Building

Advisers can best help their clients avoid the pitfalls of investing if the relationship is built on mutual trust. Unfortunately, the investor's perception of the financial services industry tends to carry over to advisers, and the main issue facing the industry is one of honesty. Accounting scandals, conflicts of interest and the bear market's attack on asset value have increased the investor's skepticism about taking an adviser's advice. When you add the fact that investors already give advisers poor marks for their ability to solve financial problems, the adviser/investor relationship appears to be on thin ice. Advisers must build trust and strong relationships with investors/clients through proper due diligence, by developing a long-term financial plan for clients, by regularly monitoring portfolio performance and by keeping in regular contact with their clients.

Establishing a relationship, building trust and planning for the long term requires that advisers understand the melding of their client's life and work. To draw clients into the planning process, an adviser needs to help them understand how to plan for the transitions of life, and how such things as marriage, buying a house, children, college and retirement impact family finances and the family's financial future. Both advisers and clients must learn to think globally; i.e., think in terms of long-term portfolio development and returns.

One valuable tool is a comprehensive investment policy statement (IPS). The IPS helps set both client expectations and actions. It can also help clients comprehend the connection between elements of the entire portfolio, rather than viewing investments individually. An occasional losing investment should be expected, and it should not launch a panic that drastically alters a portfolio's balance and asset allocation.

Developing a foundation of trust is not easy in today's market environment. In fact, many investors express dissatisfaction with their financial advisers. When asked why they stayed with the adviser, many investors assumed that alternative advisers were no better, so they stayed put. But regular and open discussions regarding return requirements, risk tolerance and portfolio decisions can inoculate both advisers and investors from hindsight and regret.

Understanding Behavioral Finance

Is there such a thing as a *rational investor?* Explaining investor behavior used to be considered a fairly straightforward task. A key assumption of many economic theories has been that all participants in the economy behave rationally. When irrational behavior was encountered, it was generally dismissed as being irrelevant.

To explain how individuals make economic decisions, economists have relied on "utility theory." Utility theory assumes that an individual's utility (level of satisfaction or value) increases with increases in wealth (i.e., more wealth is preferred to less wealth), and the more wealth you have, the less risk averse you will be. The problem is that people don't always behave this way.

In fact, an emerging field of psychological study, "behavioral finance," offers a better insight into why people behave the way they do. Also known as "behavioral economics," the term refers to the convergence of psychology and financial theory. Behavioral finance is based on the works of Dr. Daniel Kahneman (2002 Nobel Prize winner in economics), Dr. Amos Tversky, Hersh Shefrin, and the extensive research of Drs. Shlomo Benartzi, Richard Thaler, Meir Statman and John Nofsinger. In short, behavioral finance is the study of why investors think and behave the way they do about money and investing. Research suggests that investors are not always rational. Indeed, they can be thoroughly irrational, emotional and, at times, even dysfunctional.

Forget about older concepts such as fear and greed, or conservative versus aggressive. Psychologists have given us a new vocabulary for describing investor behavior. Enter the brave new world of *"myopic loss aversion, mental accounting, overconfidence, regret syndrome, cognitive dissonance, and attachment bias."* We have even been introduced to the notion that losing money hurts 2.25 times more than gaining money satisfies.[2]

There is no doubt that experts are on to something. They correctly question the illogical, such as: What compels people to drive 30 minutes to use a $1 coupon; wash their car to save $10, but never dream of washing a neighbor's car for $10; why missing a train by one minute is so much more painful than missing it by half an hour; or why the same person who would never buy the most expensive orange juice at the grocery store has no trouble plopping down $5 for a fancy designer coffee?

Behavioral finance can be quite complex. But summarizing behavioral principles have emerged that should prove helpful to investors and advisers in planning the financial future. These principles are:

• Do not try this alone.
• What you do not see can help you.
• Do not peek — stay focused.
• Maximize qualified plan contributions.
• Regularly increase your savings rate.

Do Not Try This Alone

Understanding the investing process becomes complex, particularly when investors' behavior, emotions and biases come into play. Research shows that when left to their own devices, investors make a multitude of mistakes: They do not properly allocate assets; they borrow against their 401(k)s; they overload their portfolios in a given sector or company, often with their employer's stock; they buy when they should sell, and sell when they should buy; and they are overly influenced by the "trend du jour."

The greatest lesson investors can take from behavioral finance is that they need the services of a financial adviser. Just as the typical patient would be considered foolish to attempt brain surgery on himself, the typical investor is equally lost in this complicated financial world. Advisers can help investors by illustrating how to establish goals, allocate assets, implement a long-term strategy, and monitor progress. Perhaps most important, an adviser can provide an objective viewpoint to help investors overcome the fear and emotion that often drives investment decisions.

What You Do Not See Can Help You

How much did you pay in taxes last year? It's a simple question, and many people will reply, "I didn't pay any taxes. I got a refund!" They believe this because the Internal Revenue Service (IRS) has engineered a tax-collection model that is well suited for accumulating money without us ever missing it — collection in advance. The IRS collects its piece of our paychecks automatically, before we have a chance to spend it.

Collection in advance can actually help you become a disciplined saver. An automatic investment plan allows investors to pay themselves first. Investments are treated as another part of their regular budget. Rather than impulsively spending extra income, an automatic investment plan forces investors to put money away over the long run. In addition, an adviser can show you how an automatic investment plan, along with dollar-cost averaging (although neither can guarantee profit or protection against loss) can help reduce mistakes and volatility within a portfolio.

Do Not Peek — Stay Focused on the Long Term

A long-term investment portfolio is like a bar of soap — the more you handle it, the smaller it can become. Dalbar, Inc.'s 2004 Quantitative Analysis of Investor Behavior shows that over the 20-year period that ended December 31, 2003, the S&P 500® Index returned 12.98 percent annually. Meanwhile, the average equity mutual fund investor earned a paltry 3.51 percent a year. More interesting, the average "market timer," the investor who actively traded in and out of different funds to capitalize on short-term fluctuations, actually lost 3.29 percent annually over the period.[3]

Behavioral finance teaches us that one of the best ways advisers can help clients is to convince them to keep the soap dish out of sight and away from the sink. Advisers can explain the importance of asset allocation, automatic rebalancing and, above all, a long-term perspective. Advisers can encourage clients to stop looking daily at account balances and market fluctuations, and agree, instead, to meet periodically to review their clients' progress.

Maximize Qualified Plan Contributions

You wouldn't turn down "free money," would you? It's amazing how many people do. The Profit Sharing/401(k) Council of America reports that 20 percent of workers fail to contribute to their employer-sponsored plans.[4] These salary-reduction plans allow employees to deposit pretax dollars into a retirement account. In addition, most plans offer employer-matched contributions.

Of course, employer contributions may be subject to certain vesting provisions. But assuming you stay on the job long enough, this is like adding "free" money to your nest egg. In addition, behavioral finance research shows that investors do not treat their 401(k)s the same way they do other investments. During the recent bear market, when investors moved large amounts of assets from equities to bonds, these same investors left their 401(k)s untouched.

Regularly Increase Your Savings

Many people believe they have completely protected themselves by locking up their money in a fixed-rate investment, perhaps one that is guaranteed by the FDIC. While the guarantee and safety may be attractive, the rate may not be. If you need $50,000 today, you may need in excess of $101,640, 25 years from now, assuming a 3 percent inflation rate.

Inflation is the reason to increase your savings rate. Maybe you are thinking you will start saving more "next year." Then work with an adviser to *commit to it in writing* or, if you can, take advantage of a savings program called Save More Tomorrow (SMarT). Created by Professor Richard Thaler of the University of Chicago and Professor Shlomo Benartzi of UCLA, SMarT lets workers agree to boost their savings contributions automatically with each annual raise. The worker signs up to have a fixed percentage of any annual salary increase put directly into the employer-sponsored plan. Studies have shown the average savings rates of SMarT plan participants jump tremendously. If such a program is not available to you, you can still bring this concept to your investment program by committing to increasing your savings rate annually.

While individual investor needs vary, behavioral finance suggests there are some investor desires that apply almost universally. Because investors are loss averse, they are concerned with protecting capital and limiting their losses. Investors naturally like the possibility of large gains. Searching the market for products that provide investors with strong upside potential combined with protection against losses may help meet such a need. The more investors and financial advisers understand how to make correct decisions, the easier they can build mutually beneficial long-term relationships.

Now that you know what to look for in a good financial adviser, you now need a comprehensive financial plan. The question here is:

What Does a Good Financial Plan Look Like?

Any financial plan must be designed to solve problems and attain well-defined goals. Plans come in various shapes and sizes, but they all rely on a certain format. They begin with "You Are Here" and they lead to "Your Goals" located a number of years down the road. No one can predict the future, but you can make some preparations for your journey along the way. The most important thing is to have a plan and to put it into action. When designing your plan, here are several questions to ask yourself and your adviser:

- *How long is my life expectancy?*
- *How much in dollars or in percentage of income per year should I save?*
- *What is a realistic rate of return to assume on my portfolio?*
- *What is the assumed rate of inflation?*
- *What plan should we put in place for a surviving spouse?*
- *What kind of lifestyle will I be able to afford in retirement? The same as I have now? Better?*
- *Do I want to leave money to heirs? To charity?*
- *Can I rely on my company's pension plan?*
- *How should my assets be allocated — equities, bonds, annuities, life insurance?*
- *Will my house or other real estate be a reliable source of retirement equity?*
- *How often should we review and/or modify the plan?*

Many more questions are involved and your situation is bound to change over the years, but a properly constructed plan is half the battle.

With 77 million Baby Boomers entering retirement within the next 10 to 20 years, the need for saving has never been greater and the challenge for advisers never bigger. Keeping your plan on track through tough times may take hard work and even some tough love, but you and your adviser will have to act as a team to guard your financial future.

Challenges and Solutions:

Some Questions and Answers About Retirement

How much do I need to receive $50,000 per year in retirement?

If you assume a four percent withdrawal rate on assets, a three percent rate of inflation and a seven percent returns rate on investments, what lump sum must you have to guarantee an income of $50,000 for 30 years? The amount is $1,168,225. Did you get the same answer? Most people's estimates are off by hundreds of thousands of dollars.

How much of my 401(k) plan is guaranteed?

Zero. Unless you have guaranteed investments in it such as FDIC-insured certificates of deposits or annuities backed by a state's insurance industry guaranty fund. These investments may not offer the higher returns you seek.

What is my retirement age?

More than half of workers think they are eligible for full benefits before they actually will be (54 percent), while another one in ten admits they do not know when they are eligible to retire. The Social Security age generally represents today's thinking on retirement.

But it's not your father's Social Security. Boomers living to age 65 will actually have to wait at least a year to receive full Social Security benefits.

Year of Birth	Full Benefits Age
1937 or earlier	65
1938	65 and 2 months
1939	65 and 4 months
1940	65 and 6 months
1941	65 and 8 months
1942	65 and 10 months
1943-1954	66
1955	66 and 2 months
1956	66 and 4 months
1957	66 and 6 months
1958	66 and 8 months
1959	66 and 10 months
1960 and later	67

Source: U.S. Social Security Administration. Available at: http://www.ssa.gov/retirechartred.htm

Is there a quick and easy way to save money now?

Win the lottery? Probably not. Try this: Saving $5 per day by not buying that latte or pack of cigarettes can yield $1,825 per year. That amount fits nicely in an IRA and as such can have tax-deferred potential growth. In 30 years, compounded annually at six percent you could have a fund of $154,763.06.[5]

---

[1] John J. Heldrich, Center for Workforce Development, Rutgers University, 2005.

[2] Amos Tuesby and Daniel Kahneman, "Loss Averson in Riskless Choice," *The Quartery Journal of Economics*, 106:4, 1991.

[3] "Dalbar Study Shows Market Timers Lose Their Money," *Dalbar, Inc*, April 1, 2004.

[4] 46th Annual Survey of Profit Sharing and 401(k) Plans, Profit Sharing and 401(k) Council of America, August 23, 2004.

[5] Bloomberg.com Retirement Calculator, not factored for inflation, taxes or withdrawals.

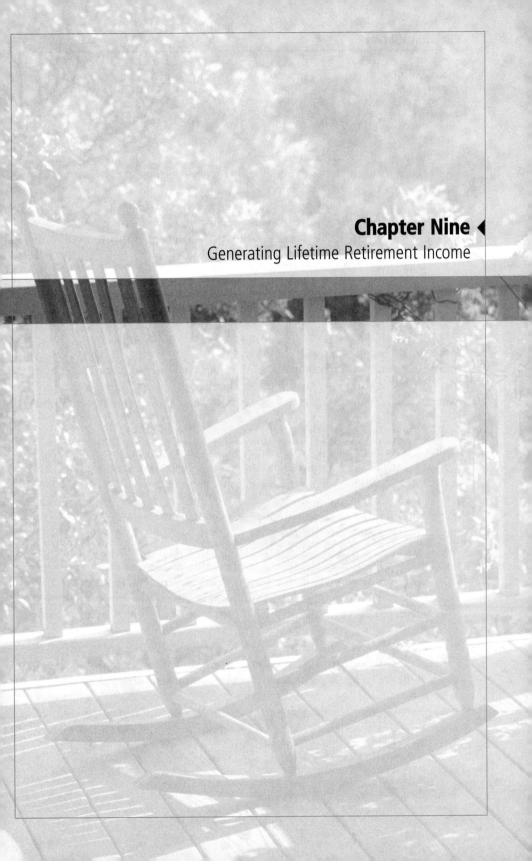

Chapter Nine ◄
Generating Lifetime Retirement Income

Each year millions of Americans enter a dramatically different phase of their lives. They transition out of the workforce and into retirement. Overnight, they move from *"accumulation"* — building wealth during their working years — to *"decumulation,"* drawing income they will need to last for the rest of their lives.

The transition into retirement requires a major change in the way people think about and manage their money. Yesterday's retirees were supported by guaranteed income sources. They could collect a pension; they could count on a Social Security check; they could depend on healthcare benefits from their employer even into retirement. Today's retirees are looking at a very different picture. They are increasingly responsible for generating their own retirement income from personal savings. At the same time, they face longer life expectancies and astounding leaps in expenses.

The fundamental principles for building and preserving wealth are well published and fairly straightforward. Start investing early; keep investing regularly; diversify your portfolio; regularly monitor your asset allocation and become more conservative as you approach retirement. Although evidence suggests most Americans are dramatically undersaved, the financial services industry has at least tried to educate the public about this *"accumulation"* phase of lifetime financial management. Accumulating assets, however, is only the first part of retirement planning.

Upon retirement, retirees must determine how to convert assets into income that can last for the rest of their lives. This process is complex and involves a long list of variables, including: when the person wants to retire; how long he or she will live; how much income will be needed; withdrawal rates; inflation; health; whether money should be passed to heirs; risk tolerance; interest rates; whether equity markets will perform poorly or positively over the next 30 years; and dozens of other considerations. The risk of making the wrong decisions is dramatically higher because retirees don't have the luxury of a long-term investment horizon to make up for any financial missteps. The financial services industry has not done a good job of helping Americans prepare for this *"decumulation"* phase of their financial lives.

One reason retirement income planning has been largely overlooked is because it is a new and difficult field for novices and investment professionals alike. An informal survey asking 25 registered representatives the following question: *"How much money would be required to provide $50,000 of annual inflation-adjusted income for 35 years assuming a 7 percent growth rate and a 3 percent rate of inflation?"* This question will typically result in 25 different, and widely discrepant, answers.

Unfortunately, planning and investment decisions based on potentially flawed "*guesstimations*" can be dangerous. Consider that according to the Department of Health and Human Services, one in ten elderly Americans live in poverty — and that number nearly doubles when the older person lives alone. We've already covered how much worse the situation could be for America's seniors if not for Social Security.

Previous chapters detail the challenges converging to create *The American Retirement Crisis*[SM]. The challenges are real and, more so than in previous generations, the responsibility for generating retirement income rests solely on each investor's shoulders. The good news is, there is hope. By understanding the challenges, you've taken a giant step in the right direction. Now it is time to put together a plan that ensures your retirement income lasts as long as you do. There are several questions you may want to keep in mind along the way:

• How much time might you spend in retirement?
• What's the *right amount* of income to withdraw from your portfolio each year?
• How is your money invested? Is your plan too aggressive or too conservative?
• Does your asset allocation mix match your risk tolerance?
• Have you thoroughly explored your future income needs?
• How much of your retirement income are you willing to leave unprotected? How much do you want to come from sources that are guaranteed?

Developing a Successful Retirement Income Plan

One way to define financial "*success*" in retirement is the ability to navigate the multitude of risks we've discussed, while being able to receive a reliable stream of lifetime income sufficient to sustain a desired lifestyle. At its highest level, retirement planning starts with three fundamental concepts: 1) timing retirement; 2) understanding withdrawal rates; and 3) properly constructing a portfolio that includes guarantees.

Timing Retirement

The single-most important retirement planning decision you will make is determining when to stop working. For decades, the clear trend in America was towards retiring earlier. In recent years, however, this trend has reversed itself and many older Americans have remained in, or returned to, the workforce to supplement their income or keep themselves busy. While a number of psychological considerations play into the retirement decision, there are an equal number of financial considerations. For the vast majority of Americans, a strictly financial evaluation of their retirement readiness will reveal the overwhelming advantages of remaining in the workforce for at least a few more years.

Today, the majority of those approaching retirement can start collecting reduced Social Security benefits at age 62 and full retirement benefits a few months after age 65. Staying on the job past age 65 provides more than three full years of additional income — and therefore potential savings. Meanwhile, your retirement nest egg remains untouched and may even grow. Delaying the retirement decision also significantly increases the "*full*" Social Security benefits you will be eligible to claim.

According to the Social Security Administration, an individual born in 1944 and now earning $50,000 could expect a monthly benefit (in 2006 dollars) of $958 on retiring at age 62; $1,350 on retiring at age 66; and $1,878 if he or she delayed retirement until age 70. This is a classic trade-off, immediate leisure versus greater future income. By age 75½, a retiree who retired at age 62 will have received virtually the same total income as a man who waited to age 66 to collect.[1] From that "*crossover*" point, however, the older retiree begins to pull ahead. Should he live to age 90, he will collect tens of thousands of dollars more from the system than the early retiree. And that doesn't count the additional income he could draw from his extra years of savings, the appreciation of untapped assets and the savings on medical insurance costs he made by working longer.

Income Streams and Withdrawal Rates

A second important decision for retirees is to determine how much money to take from their investment portfolio. The annual rate of withdrawals can, of course, dramatically raise or lower your portfolio's prospects of lasting longer.

The withdrawal rate decision depends largely on what other sources of income may be available. If you have sufficient guaranteed income in the form of pensions and Social Security benefits, you may not be as dependent on personal savings and investments. However, for the vast majority of Americans, guaranteed income sources are disappearing, meaning there is a high likelihood that you will need to convert at least a portion of your savings into retirement income.

So how much income can you afford to take from your nest egg once you retire? It was easy to be optimistic about retirement income in the late 1990s. Many investors' portfolios just seemed to go up and up. Buoyed by their swollen investments, many investors became convinced they could sustain withdrawal rates of seven percent or greater each year, and count on rising stock prices to keep the total value of their portfolios virtually unchanged or even growing. Americans were in love with the market. Then the bubble burst. The worst bear market (2000-2002) since the Great Depression brought investors back to reality. Many who had retired began reducing their budgets, changing their lifestyles, and even returning to the workforce to cope with their newfound financial shortfalls.

The following chart looks at the impact that a range of inflation-adjusted withdrawal rates would have had on a $1,000,000 portfolio of 50 percent stocks, 40 percent bonds and 10 percent short-term investments over the period from 1970 to 2004. This period includes the great bull market of the 1980s–1990s, two of the worst bear markets in Wall Street history, two major wars, two attempts to impeach U.S. Presidents, multiple recessions, and some of the the worst inflationary outbreaks in U.S. history.

What a difference 1% makes.

How Long Will It Take To Run Out Of Money

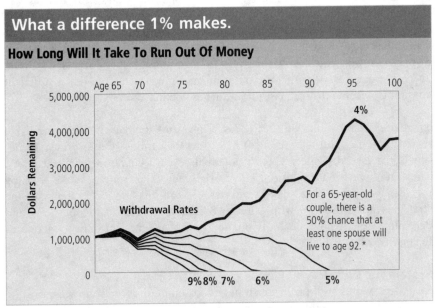

Hypothetical value of an untaxed portfolio composed of: 50% stocks as represented by the S&P 500; 40% bonds as represented by U.S. intermediate government bonds; and 10% short-term investments as measured by the U.S. 30-day Treasury Bill. Annual inflation-adjusted withdrawals based on rates specified. This hypothetical illustration uses historical performance and inflation rates from 1970 through 2004. Assumes reinvestment of dividends and interest. Chart is for illustrative purposes only and is not representative of the future performance of any particular portfolio or security. Investors cannot invest directly in an index. Past performance is no guarantee of future results.
Source: Ibbotson Presentation Materials, ©Ibbotson Associates, Inc. All rights reserved. Used with permission.
*Probability of a couple surviving based on Annuity 2000 Mortality Table from Society of Actuaries. Figure assumes a person is in good health.

As you can see, the initial pool of $1,000,000 could be exhausted within 20 years if funds were drawn down at a six percent clip. A more modest five percent withdrawal rate could have extended income from the portfolio for just over 25 years. In stark contrast, a four percent withdrawal rate — $40,000 in the first year, adjusted upwards in later years for *actual, historical inflation* — could have done more than just sustain the portfolio.

Although a four percent withdrawal rate doesn't provide any guarantee, and future results will depend on interest rates and market performance, it is clear that withdrawal rates above four percent can significantly increase the risk of running out of money.

Constructing Your Portfolio to Include Guarantees

Despite the risks outlined in this book, your retirement will very likely include some minimum level of reliable income. Most retirees and near retirees will receive at least minimal Social Security benefits for the foreseeable future. You might also receive regular income streams in the form of a corporate pension or from other interests such as rental property. After that, however, you are on your own. For the first time in your life, you will be responsible for your own paycheck, and for ensuring that your other accumulated investments provide a sufficient amount of income that can last for as long as you live.

There are several strategies and classes of investments that can provide reliable income you need during retirement. Certainly the various options present trade-offs in the forms of safety, growth potential, level of guarantees, and flexibility. The fact is, no single solution will be right for every retiree. While working together with a qualified financial adviser, you can mix and match the following strategies in accordance with your own individual goals and objectives and determine exactly how much of your retirement income you want to guarantee for the rest of your life.

Systematic Withdrawal Plans

Systematic withdrawal plans are strategies for taking income from your existing portfolio over a specific, predetermined period of time. While there are many ways to structure systematic withdrawals, most retirement portfolios can facilitate such a plan. Systematic withdrawal plans provide tremendous flexibility in terms of how much you withdraw each year, and how your rate of withdrawals can change in future years. Unfortunately, with most systematic withdrawal plans, you will be forced to continually monitor your account value and make difficult calculations and determinations about how much money you can take in a given year based on current and anticipated investment performance.

Immediate Annuities

In exchange for a nonrefundable onetime investment, immediate annuities provide a guaranteed stream of income that can last for a predetermined number of years, or for as long as you live. Ensuring a guaranteed lifetime income with an immediate annuity involves a significant trade-off. You give up access to your money in exchange for the comfort of a guaranteed regular paycheck. While this relative lack of flexibility may not be appropriate for your entire retirement portfolio, it can make immediate annuities a valuable component of your plan to ensure guaranteed income to cover at least your essential expenses.

Deferred Annuities

Deferred annuities — fixed, fixed index, and variable annuities — are increasingly popular options for retirees looking to continue to expose their portfolio to growth potential while providing the opportunity for valuable income benefits, including income that can never be outlived.

Deferred annuities are contracts sold by insurance companies that allow your money the opportunity to continue to grow without you having to pay tax on your earnings until you withdraw them. Your ability to delay paying taxes on earnings can keep more of your money working for you each year, potentially helping you accumulate more money throughout your retirement. Deferred annuities may be converted to streams of income — similar to immediate annuities.

Fixed and fixed index annuities typically provide some minimum level of interest and can provide safety for your principal during retirement. By comparison, variable annuities allow you to invest in a variety of investment options — ranging from conservative to aggressive — that may expose your money to more risk and the potential for additional reward. As with any investment in securities, variable annuities are subject to investment risks and may lose value.

Some newer variable annuities offer a variety of innovative features that can protect your principal, lock-in gains, if any, on a regular basis, and even provide a minimum level of guaranteed income that can last for the rest of your life without requiring you to annuitize your contract or lose control of your accumulated assets.

Among the most popular living benefits are Guaranteed Minimum Income Benefits (GMIB) and Guaranteed Minimum Withdrawal Benefits (GMWB), which are typically available for an additional fee. According to the National Association for Variable Annuities (NAVA), it is the provision of guaranteed lifetime income and retirement security that makes variable annuities attractive as part of a retirement income stream. From a Baby Boomer's perspective, financial advisers and companies that offer more personalized products with increased levels of customization and more choices are ones that can give you retirement income solutions that can fit your retirement income needs.

The transition from full-time work and the accumulation of assets to retirement and "decumulation" of your retirement portfolio brings on a new and complex set of financial challenges. The primary goal — achieving lifetime income — is critical. It is also very possible. Working with a financial professional, you can use a combination of investment, income and insurance products to devise a retirement income plan that will meet your retirement lifestyle. However, the most important step is often the toughest, and that is to begin the process and start working with a financial professional today.

A Step-by-Step Approach to Retirement Income Planning

Step 1: Review all income sources	• Review a list of all sources of income — Social Security, traditional pensions, lifetime annuities or other predictable long-term income flows. • Do an inventory of all financial and real assets (stocks, bonds, mutual funds, CDs, real estate, rents, etc.) that could be used to fund your retirement.
Step 2: Review all expenses	• Estimate monthly or annual expenses — dividing them into "essential" (food, housing, clothing, healthcare costs, insurance, gas, etc.) and "discretionary" (travel, entertainment, etc.).
Step 3: Compare dependable income with essential expenses	• Compare your projected essential expenses with projected total after-tax income. • This comparison will either show that your essential expenses are fully taken care of, or it will reveal an "essential expense gap" — which needs to be filled.
Step 4: Allocate assets to cover essentials and to fund discretionary expenses	• Should there be any gap in income coverage for your essential expenses, close this gap — by either segregating a specific pool of assets to draw on systematically over time or by purchasing a guaranteed income product, such as an immediate annuity — to help ensure that essential expenses are met. • Once essentials are funded, the assets remaining may be used for discretionary expenses.
Step 5: Monitor and regularly review your plan	• Review your plan with a financial professional at least once a year, adjusting all elements — including expenses, asset allocation and withdrawal rates — to meet changing personal circumstances.

One Baby Boomer's Story —

"I'll never forget the day: January 7, 2000. That's when I decided to get out of the stock market. I beat the crowd and beat the bear market. And I owe it all to teamwork," says Carl Walsh, a mortgage banker in Hermosa Beach, California.

Born on the tail end of the Baby Boom in 1957, Carl has fully participated in the economy's ups and downs from the late '70s through today. He's seen the prosperity boom beginning in the '80s, a few recessions along the way, and then the biggest bear market since the Great Depression. "Most of my investments are in real estate because that's the business I'm in," he remarks. "You're going to see some opportunities pop up from this vantage point. But I've invested in the stock market; I've had my employees' 401(k) to worry about; I've had family insurance matters; and, last but certainly not least, my retirement."

Even though traditional retirement age is several years down the road, Carl is thinking ahead. "I know what a lot of Boomers have been through," says the youngest of five children. "Even though I'm financially secure right now I still worry. In this business you see a lot of ups and downs. Interest rates go up when the economy's good, then they go down and make your products attractive, or the rates keep going down leading to a recession."

As for retirement, "I'm just a natural worrier. I've been in sales since I graduated from business school, and I still think that you're only as good as your next sale. In my field there are a lot of single transactions. It's not like I get monthly residuals from the loans I fund. I do get repeat business — new mortgages or refinancing — but it's cyclical and not predictable. It's always on to the next transaction." You don't build a lot of equity in a business like this. If I tried to sell it, what would I get?"

Carl continues, "I worry a lot, so the 'running-scared' theme of my life is actually my comfort zone. I always imagine that I could lose everything tomorrow. Instead of making me panic, that thought motivates me to plan for the future. What if I really *did* lose everything tomorrow? I've got a great wife and two kids and a dog and a house to consider. I have to think about all the things that come with responsibility."

But worry is not a bad thing when it leads to action. "The worry keeps me motivated to think about my future. The key to planning is to develop a team. I played on sports teams in high school and college, mostly hockey, lacrosse, and cross-country. Whether I was a team leader or not, I relied on my teammates, and made sure they could rely on me."

Carl's career began in the late '70s. "I graduated from college in 1979, the year of 'Malaise.' The job market was about as cold as the weather in Vermont, so I hibernated a bit at grad school and got an MBA in 1981. I rejoined the job market in the Northeast, and wouldn't you know it? Another recession. My eldest brother told me the New York and New England areas of my upbringing were becoming the 'Rust Belt,' so I headed west."

"My brother-in-law gave me the idea to 'Start big, then go small.' That is, try to sign on with a large corporation and learn the ins and outs of that business. Then take what you've learned and either find a position with a smaller company or start your own business. When I came to L.A., I was hired by a major computer firm known for its training programs. After they went to a lot of cost to train me, they decided to 'downsize' their sales force, so I didn't even have to feel guilty about my plan to leave them for a smaller company.

"I met two businessmen who were mortgage brokers, intent on forming a new firm. They seemed to be very successful and yet they were starting a business and taking some big risks. I became a partner in their new firm. My plan was to learn from the best and go out on my own in two years. A couple of years went by and, sure enough, I learned a lot. One of the things I learned was that I was the only salesman and I was producing all of the firm's income! I could improve my commissions just by taking 100 percent instead of the split with the office. I was ready to do it, and the rest, as they say, is history."

Carl's place in the Baby Boom is seven years from its end in 1964. Still he knows that many of his fellow boomers have not saved nearly enough for retirement. "If I could advise other investors," he says, "I'd say that if you can start your own business there are so many more ways to accumulate retirement dollars than any other avenue. The amount you can shelter is so much greater than in a garden-variety IRA or corporate 401(k). Depending on whether you have a lot of employees, your risk of starting a business can be rewarded with long-term retirement savings."

"If you think it's too late to start a business," he continues, "then find someone who has it figured out. A good financial adviser is worth his or her weight in gold. Get some good people on your team and pull together. If you're in a two-earner family, try to trim your lifestyle to live on one income and save the other earner's checks each month. Maximize all the IRA and workplace matches and shelters available."

"Like me," he concludes, "you *should* worry about the future. You'll be more likely to take action and get your retirement plan in order. Just roll up your sleeves and go to work."

---

[1] Social Security Administration Benefits Calculator (www.ssa.gov/planners/calculators.htm).

Epilogue

The American retirement crisis is a train wreck ready to happen. Imagine a train carrying 77 million Baby Boomers toward retirement and on the same track, coming from the opposite direction, another train carrying under-funded pension promises, shrinking Social Security benefits and rising healthcare costs. Unable to stop either train, a serious crash seems inevitable. Even Baby Boomers who have diligently saved over the years are fearful of getting caught in such a tangled mess. But is it really inevitable?

It seems clear that you will spend more time in retirement than your parents did. It also seems clear that many of you have not put away enough savings to support your retirement years. And the things you were counting on to support you — pension plans, Social Security and personal savings — are not as secure and trustworthy as they used to be. In fact, most of the burden of saving for retirement has shifted away from your employers and the government to you. But research and market experience with investing suggest that you are your own worst enemy when it comes to building retirement savings through investments. And at least 40 percent of you haven't even started to save for retirement.

Taxes, inflation and healthcare are other stumbling blocks to a secure retirement. Taxes and inflation can be satisfactorily handled, but not without planning. It is healthcare that frightens people in retirement and those approaching retirement. Even those who have managed to save and build substantial nest eggs are insecure when it comes to the impact of healthcare on retirement income. Increases in health costs threaten to eat up Social Security benefits for retirees, and will probably make a sizeable dent in the incomes of wealthier retirees, especially if they have to spend part of their retirement years in a nursing home or have home care.

To put it simply, there is a crisis, but few of you are in crisis mode.

Lack of Information and Planning

Until now, many of you were unaware of the impending retirement crisis and the factors contributing to it. Using your parents as examples, most of you assumed that your retirement years would be like your parents' retirement, only better. Once you had put in your years of work — making contributions to your pension plans, Social Security and individual retirement accounts — you would retire to a comfortable, leisurely life and enjoy your Golden Years. Perhaps you would even retire earlier than your parents had. Lacking any information to the contrary, you assumed that everything was right with your retirement. But underneath the surface, the elements of a sound, successful retirement were showing cracks in their foundations, and soon they would begin to crumble, threatening your future.

Given your self-assurance, confidence and heavy reliance on employers and the government for much of your retirement income, you seem to have been lulled into complacency about the need to plan for retirement. Without a sense of urgency, a need to save for the future gave way to a consumption mentality, which eventually created a huge debt burden for many of you. The frugal nature of your parents was replaced with a desire to own as many material things as possible, even if it meant borrowing or spending beyond what you actually earned. Little, if any, thought was given to developing a retirement plan or increasing your level of savings to ensure a secure future. Even those of you who had an active propensity to invest did so not to secure your future, but to make more money for the present or the short-term future. Very few members of your enormous demographic group engaged in serious retirement planning. And those who did were focused on asset accumulation.

Not until after the bear market of 2000-2002 did it become apparent that you were headed for a retirement that could potentially be worse than your parents'. The spread of information concerning the nature of the crumbling legs of the retirement stool painted a different picture of the future for you. Your self-assurance and confidence began to turn to worry, anxiety and downright fear. Those safe, secure defined benefit pension plans were in decline, and many were seriously under-funded by employers. As information about people living longer emerged, it became apparent that retirees would soon outnumber workers, which meant that less money was being contributed to government entitlement programs as more was being withdrawn. Without change, entitlement programs would bottom out, ending benefits meant for retirement. To save these programs would require either tax increases or benefit cuts, both of which meant lower retirement incomes for you. What had appeared to be a rather pleasant ending to a fruitful life now seemed rather dismal. For the first time in your lives, you contemplated the prospect of not having enough money for your retirement years.

Unfortunately, many of you, who grew up during a time of relative economic prosperity, have not shared your parents' attitude of saving and financial prudence. When you look back, you may see lost years, sometimes two and three decades, where few, if any, assets were put away for the future. If you missed out on years of compounding interest, you are hardly in a position to make up the difference during the few remaining years before retirement. It's little wonder that our nation's retirement confidence is lagging.

Perhaps the biggest stumbling block is fear of planning. Part of this comes from an attitude of procrastination and not wanting to face up to the task, but another part is a lack of information. This fuels a lack of confidence. A recent survey by Transamerica suggests that 50 percent of the respondents agreed they would like to receive more information and advice. In fact, they would prefer to rely on outside experts to monitor and manage their retirement investments. They simply don't know as much as they should about retirement planning and investing.[1] But the trick is to overcome the fear and take the first step toward the solution.

Taking Charge

The responsibility for your financial future in retirement lies with you. Until now, many of you have ignored your future, preferring to spend assets in the present rather than save them for the future. Now that retirement is more real to you, there is increasing concern about whether or not there will be enough money for retirement. This situation is not going to change unless you take charge and do something about it.

Since your retirement can take multiple paths, you need the advice of a professional who can help determine which path is right for you. Don't rely on your own instincts. Find a financial professional who is truly concerned about your needs, ambitions and retirement plan. Since you are placing your retirement and your financial future in an adviser's hands, you must find someone you can trust. Trust and relationship comfort are critical dimensions; you must be able to take this adviser's advice and follow it. If you are not comfortable doing that, then you need to keep looking.

Finally, once a plan is in place, follow it. You've paid the adviser to help you analyze your retirement needs and goals, and the two of you have come up with a plan to reach them. If something feels wrong, discuss it with your adviser. Make use of his or her knowledge. Together, the two of you have a much better chance of making the appropriate decision than you do by yourself.

Plan your retirement but never retire your plan.

---

[1] "Transamerica Survey Shows Lack of Confidence and Knowledge in Retirement Savings," *Insurance Newscast,* March 10, 2006.

Index